Imagining Incest

Imagining Incest

Sexton, Plath, Rich, and Olds on Life with Daddy

Gale Swiontkowski

SUP

Selinsgrove: Susquehanna University Press
London: Associated University Presses

Associated University Presses
2010 Eastpark Boulevard
Cranbury, NJ 08512

Associated University Presses
Unit 304
The Chandlery
50 Westminster Bridge Road
London SE1 7QY, England

Associated University Presses
P.O. Box 338, Port Credit
Mississauga, Ontario
Canada L5G 4L8

The paper used in this publication meets the requirements of the American National Standard for Permanence of Paper for Printed Library Materials Z39.48-1984.

Acknowledgments appear on pages 15–16.

Library of Congress Cataloging-in-Publication Data

Swiontkowski, Gale
    Imagining incest : Sexton, Plath, Rich, and Olds on life with daddy / Gale Swiontkowski.
        p.   cm.
    Includes bibliographical references and index.
    ISBN 1-57591-061-6 (alk. paper)
    1. American poetry—Women authors—History and criticism.   2. Women and literature—United States—History—20th century.   3. American poetry—20th century—History and criticism.   4. Rich, Adrienne Cecile—Criticism and interpretation.   5. Plath, Sylvia—Criticism and interpretation.   6. Sexton, Anne—Criticism and interpretation.   7. Olds, Sharon—Criticism and interpretation.   8. Fathers and daughters in literature.   9. Incest in literature.   I. Title.
PS151.S94   2003
811'.54093520431—dc21   2003001298

To JNC

"Speech, after long silence; it is right. . . ."
—W. B. Yeats

Contents

Preface:
Some Cautions and Many Thanks

I FEEL I NEED TO POST A WARNING AT THE BEGINNING OF THIS BOOK, SIMI-
lar to the disclaimer found at the beginning of many works of fiction
these days: "Any resemblance between characters and situations in
this book and real people and events is entirely accidental and unin-
tentional." The reasons such a disclaimer seem necessary to this
work of literary criticism are two: the fundamentally fictional nature
of poetry (even of the "confessional" poetry that will be studied
here), and the socially controversial nature of the main topic of this
book, father-daughter incest. Anyone who has read Janet Malcolm's
The Silent Woman, on the conflicts between Sylvia Plath's biographers
and those who have managed Plath's estate since her death, will be
aware of grave concerns for the reputations of deceased writers by
members of their families, as well as similar concerns for the surviving family members themselves. I respect those concerns and wish
to state clearly here that I intend to explore symbolic motifs in
poetry, not the actual experiences of the poets themselves, and that
I have no intent to apply poetic themes to biographies. Let me state
my case even more directly: father-daughter incest is not part of my
own personal history, nor do I assume it to be the actual experience
of the four poets I study here. In fact, it will become clear in my
discussions of the poetry that the incestuous Daddy figure, established by Sexton and Plath and revised by Rich and Olds, is *not* iden-
tical to the biological fathers of these four women. This Daddy is a
shared archetype, a symbolic embodiment of one form of communal experience. Certainly, the poets' experiences with their real
fathers influenced their later creation and revision of the poetic
Daddy, but that poetic figure is symbolic also of social experiences
that extend well beyond the poets' first-loved males. The Daddy figure is representative in that larger sense because, paradoxically, he
emerges from the emotionally subjective and symbolic realm of the
psyche and not from an objective account of history.

9

It is worth noting what C. G. Jung once said of the creation of incest images in the psyche: "the whole drama takes place in the individual's own psyche, where the 'parents' are not the parents at all but only their imagoes . . . representations which have arisen from the conjunction of parental peculiarities with the individual disposition of the child" (1980, 5:328). Jung is speaking here of incest fantasies, not of memories of actual events; for this reason, what he says is also relevant to parental imagery in poetry. Imagoes are internal, psychic images that embody personal experience as it has intersected with more universal human experiences. The mother and father imagoes we carry inside ourselves as adults have been enhanced over time to reflect our experiences of figures in society who play mother and father roles for us, as well as our experiences of our own parents. Sylvia Plath once spoke of the representative, social nature of personal experience in poetry, thereby explaining why her poetic Daddy (unlike her personal father) is, in part, a Nazi: "I think that personal experience is very important, but certainly it shouldn't be a kind of shut-box and mirror-looking, narcissistic experience. I believe it should be relevant, and relevant to the larger things, the bigger things such as Hiroshima and Dachau and so on" (1966, 169–70).

Anne Sexton similarly stated on several occasions that even when her poetry sounds most personal and in fact deals with real personal issues, it is still not autobiographical fact and can not be: "Poetic truth is not necessarily autobiographical. It is truth that goes beyond the immediate self, another life. I don't adhere to literal facts all the time; I make them up whenever needed. Concrete examples give a verisimilitude" (1985, 103). Poetry is fiction and not fact, for it intentionally reshapes and colors the raw materials of experience. This is as true for confessional poetry as it is for dramatic monologues by fictional characters. Notably, Sexton never chose to write an autobiography in which she could have clarified for those who wished to know, or even perhaps for herself, her own personal experiences with her father. She did choose to explore many different facets of the incest motif in her poems, through what seems at times to be her own voice and through the voices of other dramatic characters. Sexton, that is, chose to open up the nuances of the incest motif in poetry and not to nail down any particular historical events. The result is a subjective exploration of psychic realities—not of actual experiences, but of personal, emotional reverberations from social experiences.

The manner in which Sexton explores this intermingling of subjective and objective experience can be seen in a poem called "The Death Baby," which includes this passage:

> . . . My sister at six
> dreamt nightly of my death:
> "The baby turned to ice.
> Someone put her in the refrigerator
> and she turned as hard as a Popsicle."

The next line is in Sexton's voice: "I remember the stink of the liverwurst . . ." (1981, 354). The hostility of a sibling, perhaps known only symbolically through the dreams she relates, is nonetheless received tangibly by the younger sister, as indeed emotional aggression is often experienced physically by its target. Even accepting that one of Sexton's older sisters felt hostility toward Anne, we don't suppose (and Sexton doesn't expect us to) that Anne wound up in the refrigerator next to the liverwurst. But Sexton does ask us to consider in reading this poem that such an image *can* be the *emotional reality* of the experience. The emotional injury was once experienced and now recurs in this immediate and literal imagery—the poet, in speaking out the child's experience, demonstrates the tendency of the psyche to preserve emotional metaphors in concrete, sensual forms.

This internal, emotional world is no less real than the rational, social world we all share, for each of us lives partly within the symbolic realm of emotional interpretations. We are always making sense of external experience inside ourselves—sometimes consciously, sometimes not. In that subjective realm the Daddy image in modern women's poetry is an accretion of woman's experiences with male authorities, from whom she wants love, favor, protection, advancement, respect, and much else, and with whom she often finds only a partial, sexualized union and rejection of or deafness to her hopes and desires. The incest motif in poetry thus embodies both the daughter's common desire for a symbolic union with her father and also the common experience of her actual subjection to or thoughtless exploitation by him or his social representatives. The inner realm of symbols is not reducible to historical fact, as our legalistic, talk-show society often wants it to be, but it is nonetheless real and compelling in its record of emotional experience. We must just remember in reading the poetry that emerges from this realm that we are *not* reading personal history.

Psychologist Otto Rank offered this caution in *The Incest Theme in Literature and Legend,* which was written over eighty years ago but is still helpful advice today:

> It is psychologically misguided to look for actual experiences in the au-
> thor's life as parallels to his literary themes, because the themes are the
> products of fantasy activity, for which actual experiences are only raw
> material subject to the most extreme modifications. (1992, 94)

Likewise, I speak purposefully in this book of the incest *motif,* by which I mean the subjective images and themes that cluster around the topic of incest in women's poetry. I have no wish to decide the question of whether or not Sexton or any other poet I discuss had an incestuous experience as a child. What is historical fact and what is imagined symbol is just not a relevant distinction in the realm of poetry, where the two are necessarily entangled. To try to define Sexton's actual childhood relations with certain family members would distract from her powerful poetic messages about the many harmful effects on women of physical and emotional incest. In each and every case, I am examining the poem and not the poet. Even when I refer to the speaker of the poem by the author's name, I am referring to the author's persona, her created voice in that poem, and making no claim for autobiographical truth.

All these cautions stated, I would propose a connection between the incest motif that persists in the poetry of many contemporary American women and the current proliferation of recovered memories of incest in many women over the past decade. In an essay entitled "Beware the Incest-Survivor Machine," in the *New York Times Book Review,* psychologist Carol Tavris warned against books for incest survivors that create their own audiences by providing long checklists of universal symptoms. She complained of those lists, "Nobody doesn't fit" (1993, 1). Tavris recognizes the real problem of incest today but also cautions that memory is a tricky business:

> Researchers who study memory and the brain are discovering the brain's
> capacity to construct and invent reality from the information it proc-
> esses. Their studies support what poets and novelists have always known:
> that memory is not a fixed thing, with its own special place or file drawer
> in the brain. It is a *process* that is constantly being reinvented. A "mem-
> ory" consists of fragments of the event, subsequent discussions and read-
> ing, other people's recollections and suggestions, and, perhaps most of
> all, present beliefs about the past. (16)

Working within this definition, I would posit that a great many women have had actual experiences of abuse in some form that, combined with their cultural conditioning, could surface in later years as memories of incest. How much of the memory is factual and how much internally constructed is almost irrelevant (outside the legal system)—the fact remains that the psychic experience is one of abuse rather than respect or nurture. Adrienne Rich has cautioned that "every journey into the past is complicated by delusions, false memories, false naming of real events" (1976, 15); however, such deceptive byways, often responses to social pressures, must be explored in order to arrive at personal truth. In the prologue to his own memoirs, Jung tries to define the symbolic or mythic reality of one's own story:

> What we are to our inward vision, and what man appears to be *sub specie aeternitatis,* can only be expressed by way of myth. Myth is more individual and expresses life more precisely than does science. . . . Whether or not the stories are "true" is not the problem. The only question is whether what I tell is *my* fable, *my* truth. (1965, 3)

What we can see and feel vicariously in the poetry of Anne Sexton, Sylvia Plath, Adrienne Rich, Sharon Olds, and other contemporary women poets should help us to understand the emotional nature of the modern female experience, since these poets are creating in their poetry a true fable, a visionary myth out of their own emotional experiences. I am a literary critic by training and not a therapist, so my reading of the poetry of these women is analytic in the critical and not the therapeutic sense. Nevertheless, I believe these women have ideas and images to pass on to us that illuminate many of our present social and psychological dilemmas, such as the explosion in the last decade of recovered memories of incest that Tavris discusses. It is true that many women *do* fit the list of symptoms of incest survivors, but rather than using the inclusive nature of the list to invalidate it, why don't we ask why so many seem to fit? Is it possible that virtually all women suffer the effects of incest, symbolic if not actual? Does such a nearly universal assessment lead necessarily to rejection or belittlement, to the conclusion that we should all grin and bear our modern female neurosis? Or might we dig for the roots of this common problem and then seek a cure? It is, after all, not just a woman's problem but a social dilemma, as we have witnessed in the social controversy that the recovery of abuse memories has generated. Tavris sees the deception of the "incest-survivor machine" as resting in a concept of healing that bypasses the need for social change: "Healing is *defined* as your realization that you were a victim of sexual abuse and that it explains everything wrong with your life. . . . [I]f the victim can fix herself, nothing [in society] has to change" (1993,17).

The poets studied in this book *do* connect incest and social responsibility; they relate incest to social power and often to affluence, the symbol of social power. Sexton's "Daddy" Warbucks supplies the money that helps to ensure Orphan Annie's compliance; the "Daddy" of Plath's poem of that name is depicted in part as a Nazi, his daughter as a Jew. In both cases, male authorities benefit socially and psychologically from conflict and from victimizing others, and women benefit secondarily only to the extent that they comply with the male authorities, their social Daddies. All children have to negotiate power relationships with their parents, but women often find that they never grow beyond their subordinate relation to their fathers, as boys do when they grow up to be the next fathers of society. Many women find that the relationship with the traditional father in a patriarchal society is reproduced in nearly every other segment of their lives that involves contact with an authority figure, from husband to boss to priest to president, even after they are grown up and supposedly independent beings. If the father remains the Daddy, so do his social surrogates. Within such a patriarchal society, incest may be seen as a lifelong emotional experience for women. According to one feminist psychologist writing not long after Sexton and Plath, emotional incest is in fact the prescribed way of life for women: "While most women do not commit incest with their biological fathers, patriarchal marriage, prostitution, and mass 'romantic' love are psychologically predicated on sexual union between Daughter and Father figures" (Chesler 1972, 20). As an example, Adrienne Rich discusses the "seductive gestures by men who have the power to award grades" to their female students: "Even if turned aside, such gestures constitute mental rape, destructive to a woman's ego. They are acts of domination, despicable as the molestation of the daughter by the father" (1979, 242–43).

No wonder so many women who have recovered memories of abuse are now publishing (making public) those memories in an attempt to expose and reject the way certain characteristics of the patriarchal system work within their psyches, even if not on their bodies. Jane Gallop has spoken of publication as an act of breaking open the otherwise closed "cell" of family secrets that disadvantages some members and advantages others: "Once published, the scandal can no longer be contained within the family. Publication 'disperses'. . . . The circle of the family is broken, the cell walls burst" (1982, 135). Rich also has spoken of the threat of publication, not only to the social structures exposed but to the writer herself:

> For a very long time, poems were a way of talking about what I couldn't talk about any other way. And why is it that you're not able to talk about certain things? It's because they are the points of danger, you feel that in the social fabric, you feel there are people who don't want you to raise this question, or—if you're a child—to ask this question. That is the threatening place, and of course it becomes a place of great fascination too. (1993b, 271)

No wonder the issue persists as a focus in women's poetry; father-daughter incest is more than a poetic motif—it is an archetype currently being confronted on a social stage.

⌒

ACKNOWLEDGMENTS

My gratitude goes first to my colleagues at Fordham University for their support during the years of writing this book, in particular those who helped with words, ideas, and even a fan during the hot summer months: John Antush, Joanne Dobson, Richard Giannone, Moshe Gold, Connie Hassett, Mike Macovski. Thanks to my students at Fordham also, whose responses to the poetry of these four women enlivened my own. John Romig Johnson and Deborah Tannen provided valued words of encouragement, as did my birth family and my friend Jim O'Gara. My deepest love goes to my sons, William and Charles, who cheered me on even though they wondered at the strange topic I chose to write on. My greatest debt is expressed in the dedication.

Excerpts from *Satan Says,* by Sharon Olds, copyright © 1980. Reprinted by permission of the University of Pittsburgh Press.
Excerpts from *The Gold Cell,* by Sharon Olds, copyright © 1987 by

Imagining Incest

Introduction:
The Enigma of Recovered Memories

THE COVER OF THE NOVEMBER 29, 1993, ISSUE OF *TIME* MAGAZINE DIS-played a portrait of Sigmund Freud with the top part of his head disintegrating into jigsaw puzzle pieces; the accompanying caption queried, "Is Freud Dead?" Inside, two rather sensational articles discussed the current troubles of the psychotherapeutic profession. In "The Assault on Freud," *Time* gasped: "The collapse of Marxism, the other giant unified theory that shaped and rattled the 20th century, is unleashing monsters. What inner horrors or fresh dreams might arise should the complex Freudian monument topple as well?" (Gray 1993, 47). And in "Lies of the Mind," *Time* reported on repressed memory therapy and false memory syndrome as phenomena that are "harming patients, devastating families, . . . and intensifying a backlash against all mental-health practitioners" (Jaroff 1993, 52). In this article, Paul McHugh, chair of the Department of Psychiatry at Johns Hopkins University, says of the recent proliferation of recovered memories of childhood sexual abuse, primarily in adult women: "It's reached epidemic proportions" (qtd. in Jaroff 1993, 52). Other unnamed "critics of the recovered-memory movement" are said to believe that "the accusations and convictions are reminiscent of the 17th century Salem witchcraft trials" (Jaroff 1993, 55).

Six months earlier, in its double issue of May 17–24, 1993, the *New Yorker* ran a two-part story by Lawrence Wright entitled "Remembering Satan" (later published as a book with the same title), which investigated in much greater depth a remarkable tale of how recovered memories of Satanic ritual abuse devastated a previously functional and even socially admirable family. Toward the end of this article as well, the issue of witch-hunting emerges in a quotation from a paper presented to the American Psychological Association by Elizabeth Loftus in 1992, but with a different twist:

Witches in New England were mostly poor women over 40 who were
misfits. . . .Today, the accused are often men of power and success. The
witch accusations of past times were more often leveled by men, but
today the accusations are predominantly leveled by women. Today's phenomenon is more than anything a movement of the weak against the
strong. There is today a "great fear" that grips our society, and that is
fear of child abuse. (qtd. in Wright 1994, 175)

The *New Yorker*'s more sensitive and detailed story allows for strong
doubt and also a recognition of need. Why are so many adult children and their parents, as well as many agents of social welfare and
protection, being drawn almost irresistibly into this dramatic social
process of telling or refuting family secrets—real or imagined, fan-
tastic or convincing—that would never have been made public on
such a scale in previous generations? This drama is not just being
played out on the pop-culture level of "Geraldo, Oprah, Sally Jessy
Raphael and other daytime TV talk shows," as *Time* reports (Jaroff
1993, 56). Many responsible therapists, social workers, and victims
are speaking openly and seriously of this "epidemic." On May 15,
1994, the *New York Times Book Review* ran a review of three books on
recovered memories, including *Remembering Satan*. The reviewer,
psychiatrist Walter Reich, wrote judiciously about the phenomenon
and the effects of "these plague years of true and false memories of
sexual abuse":

> It's not known how many incidents of real sexual abuse take place each
> year or how many of the charges of sexual abuse turn out to be false.
> Nor is it known how much damage the false charges cause to those
> against whom they're made, to those who make them, to the families
> within which they're made and to the real victims whose accounts of sex-
> ual abuse are greeted with skepticism as a result of the growing revela-
> tions of false charges. (1994, 1, 33)

In the October 31, 1993, issue of the *New York Times Magazine*,
Linda Katherine Cutting, a concert pianist and novelist, reveals her
incestuous childhood relationship with her clergyman-father and
her mother's refusal to protect her. She concludes with what appears to be the reason she wrote this article: "I told my parents I
would no longer remain silent about the incest. I told them I would
no longer accept lingerie gifts from the father who molested me and
the mother who ignored my pleas for help" (1993, 54). Cutting's
revelations joined many other reports over the preceding years of

the sexual abuse of young men and especially women by parents, religious leaders, teachers, day-care providers: some substantiated, some withdrawn or disproved. There is certainly a crisis occurring in this country, but it's not a crisis only of recovered memories and the question of their legitimacy. It seems, more broadly, to be a crisis of faith in authority. What the accusers of child abuse agree on, whether their memories of abuse are verifiable or not, is that traditional authority figures have become profoundly suspect—and the most revered authorities, at that: not only the father and the priest as selfish abusers but also the mother as cowardly abettor, if not an abuser in her own right.

Leonard Shengold, a Freudian analyst who works with adult survivors of childhood abuse, suggests there is an analogy between growing social recognition of what can and does occur between parent or parent-surrogate and child and what has happened on a global basis in recent history: "Child abuse is the abuse of power. . . . Soul murder has a particular resonance with the twentieth century" (1989, 3). Sylvia Plath, in her conjunctions of father-Nazi, daughter-Jew in the poem "Daddy," would seem to agree. Feminist psychiatrist Judith Lewis Herman asserts that the abuse of social power is particularly evident in father-daughter incest:

> Father-daughter incest is not only the type of incest most frequently reported but also represents a paradigm of female sexual victimization. The relationship between father and daughter, adult male and female child, is one of the most unequal relationships imaginable. It is no accident that incest occurs most often precisely in the relationship where the female is most powerless. . . . The horror of incest is not in the sexual act, but in the exploitation of children and the corruption of parental love. (1992, 4)

Herman has also developed the analogy between private and public forms of violence: "There is a war between the sexes. Rape victims, battered women, and sexually abused children are its casualties. Hysteria is the combat neurosis of the sex war" (32). Cultural critic James Twitchell agrees that reports of incest are almost epidemic, but he qualifies that observation with this one: "incest in America is almost plaguelike in our collective imaginations" (1987, 13)—that is, the incest phenomenon is not just actual but also symbolic. Twitchell devotes the first two chapters of his book on the cultural motif of incest to analyzing the prevalence of incest themes and im-

ages in the high art and popular culture of the modern era. His commentary on the not-too-veiled use of incest imagery in advertising,
movies, and other video media is particularly revealing; it becomes
clear that incest sells well in this country at this time. It seems quite
possible that there are correspondences among our growing awareness of actual occurrences of incest, our subliminal cultural obses-
sion with symbolic incest, and the highly conscious and publicized
phenomenon of recovered memories of incest.

Twitchell reproduces a magazine ad that seems particularly relevant to the controversy over recovered memories of incest. In this
1984 advertisement for a brand of sweaters, a photo of a woman in
her twenties with long blond hair, a ruffled-neck blouse, a long
string of pearls, an embroidered sweater, and a rather self-satisfied
smile is presented beneath this caption: "Eunice simply had to bor-
row Mummy's Braemar sweater for her interview. At Daddy's bank"
(Twitchell 1987, 30). The ad is rife with insinuations of an incestuous hoarding of money and social position within a family of privilege, which cultural anthropologist Claude Lévi-Strauss sees as the
originating necessity for the incest taboo (to be discussed in chapter
2). But to Eunice and all other young women today conditioned by
such social imagery, the message is dismal. The end of maturation
for women of privilege in this culture like Eunice is not some degree
of independence or free thought and action, but what might easily
be called an incestuous absorption into an extended family system.
Eunice does not leave her parents and discover her own talents and
career; she remains Mummy and Daddy's little girl. She has grown
into Mummy's expensive sweater, her uniform of social maturity,
and she becomes the helpmate of Daddy, who is so busy preserving
and extending the family fortune. Eunice simply extends her mother's role—she becomes the junior wife. She could easily be the
speaker of Anne Sexton's "'Daddy' Warbucks," if she were able to
speak her feelings.

It seems almost incomprehensible that any industry would wish to
engender such subliminal associations of incest with its product,
until one realizes that the ad is aimed at the wealthy and that incest
itself is a form of hoarding. This ad and many others like it constitute an important visual segment of our culture, subconsciously conditioning young women to assume their proper role in a society of
affluence. Twitchell very interestingly demonstrates that in the past
folk stories and Gothic novels served a similar function in educating
young girls, but in those cases the coded message was to avoid incest

(1987,152ff.). What is most striking about modern advertisements carrying allusions to incest is that they often use the theme of incest as a lure to sell their product—they encourage rather than discourage incestuous fantasies. Twitchell notes a similar romantic affirmation of father-daughter incest in the realm of popular music: "We have a multitude of folk, popular, and country and western songs addressed to 'baby' or 'daddy' that play off the emotional spark of displaced fathers and daughters" (1987, 53).

So the society that responds with confusion and horror to an "epidemic" of recovered memories of incest in their grown daughters has also utilized the economic benefits of symbolic incest in its own popular culture. At a time when a children's video game called Night Trap, which featured "five scantily clad women [who] are stalked down by bloodthirsty vampires who like to drill holes in their victims' necks and hang them on meat hooks," could be developed and marketed (Elmer-DeWitt 1993, 70–71), is it really surprising that women, the targets of such violent cultural fantasies, will recall or fantasize in turn the psychological and physical assault of incest? Lawrence Wright has noted that the "imagery of babies being cut up and sacrificed" that often occurs in recovered memories of satanic ritual abuse greatly resembles the photos of mutilated fetuses that are "a prominent feature of antiabortion protest," and he speculates that "the psychic damage done by the abortion debate is reflected in the anguished fantasies of so many young women" (1994, 198). If father-daughter incest is a transgression of social responsibility by the paternal authority for primitive personal gratification at the expense of the daughter's personal integrity, then incest is occurring not only in reality but also in cultural symbolism with great frequency. That some women are recovering real memories of physical incest, that some are recovering scenarios that may have developed in response to cultural conditioning, and that many will grapple with a confusion of the two situations is inevitable—clearly, incest both really occurs in many individual cases and is symbolically touted in modern American society generally. There are many shades of gray. To cite Twitchell once again: "The unravelling of incest motifs often unfolds what Lacanians refer to as the mirror-imaging of the self, a reflection of knowledge about the self as well as an image of the magnified self, society itself" (1987, 106).

Perhaps recovered incest images in part reflect the still deeply and oppressively patriarchal nature of our society, which Adrienne Rich has most compellingly characterized from a feminist perspective:

Patriarchy is the power of the fathers: a familial, social, ideological, political system in which men—by force, direct pressure, or through ritual, tradition, laws and language, customs, etiquette, education, and the division of labor, determine what part women shall or shall not play, and in which the female is everywhere subsumed under the male. . . . The power of the fathers has been difficult to grasp because it permeates everything, even the language in which we try to describe it. (1976, 57–58)

The crisis of recovered memories of incestuous abuse can be seen as part of a quarrel within an extended patriarchal family, and some of those who believe and support the women who are recovering such memories characterize the shocked responses of many social authorities as an angry retort in this intimate disagreement. *Time* thus reports the opinion of Christine Courtois, author of several books on sexual abuse, that "the 'wholesale degradation of psychotherapy by some critics' . . . represents 'displaced rage' at therapists for bringing the issue to public attention" (Jaroff 1993, 55). Interestingly, in the first court verdict in favor of a parent suing for damages against therapists he believed wrongly influenced his daughter to "remember" fantastical incidents of incest, the jury awarded the father $500,000 for lost income and discredited the continuing allegations of sexual abuse by the daughter (Ayres 1994). Such support for the paternal defendant at the expense of the younger female plaintiff is the common patriarchal response to incest allegations, as documented by Herman and Hirschman (1982, 164ff.). Not surprisingly, the "truth" of the father presides in a patriarchal society, and the monetary compensation for his daughter's challenge to his truth carries out the link of incest and affluence proffered by the advertising media. Jacqueline Rose has cast more light on this extended family argument in her discussion of the vexed relations among Plath scholars and the keepers of the Plath estate:

It is as if the refusal of the various protagonists to recognize falseness, uncertainty, multiplicity of often incompatible points of view, as a property of language and psyche, leads them all to engage in a battle to locate it somewhere, thereby turning it into an exclusively ethical problem, on condition that it does not implicate—contaminate—any of the protagonists themselves.

In this context, to own the facts of one's own life is not self-evidence, it is *war*—a war in which the husbands and wives, mothers and daughters battle over the possession of—or rather, the constitution of what will pass as the truth. (1991, 76)

Incest is as old as the family itself, so why is this grand-scale family argument going public now? Herman argues that patriarchal societies repress knowledge of incest for vast periods of time, so that communal consciousness of it surfaces only at times of social upheaval and challenge to the status quo. In *Trauma and Recovery*, Herman presents the parallel histories of post-traumatic stress disorders in male war veterans and in female survivors of domestic violence, writing of the nineteenth-century diagnosis of "hysteria" in women, of "shell shock" in soldiers between World War I and the Vietnam War, and of sexual violence in the present day (1992, 9). As Herman's survey shows, the "reality" of incest depends on the current relationship between the individual and the society she lives in. A challenge within a society to the traditional authorities of that society enables the victims of the status quo to reveal their sufferings; they have a context in which to speak and be heard. At other times, when the authorities are not seriously questioned, the victims are silenced; there is no audience for their stories. According to Herman's analysis, we are now in the midst of a long-term feminist challenge to the patriarchal status quo, which is creating a context in which women can speak of their injuries within that social structure. (For further feminist discussion of the "memory wars," see Clegg 1999; Showalter 1997; and Wilson 1999.)

In dealing with the topic of incest, therefore, one must consult not only current reports but also the history of incest as it has been recorded both outwardly, in social responses to it, and inwardly, in the psyches of individuals. Although this book will focus primarily on the poetry of four modern American women who deal in different ways with incest themes and images, chapter 2 will examine some of the prominent modern psychological and sociological theories on incest in order to assess the cultural climate in which modern women have been writing and trying to define themselves. It will become clear that the fields of psychology and sociology have not been much more unified in their understandings of incest than are the women currently seeking to make sense of recovered memories of incest. This detour from literary criticism becomes clearly necessary following chapter 1, a study of the unresolved incest problem in the poetry of Anne Sexton and Sylvia Plath, who were writing during the time those theories had their greatest impact on society. In addition, each chapter that considers modern women poets will also refer to a traditional story from our cultural past that has previously dealt with the issue in similar symbolic terms: for Sexton and Plath, the tale of Electra; for Rich, the recreated "history" of Sappho; for Olds, the apocryphal accounts of Sophia. Considered within this larger historical and cultural context, one might say that the confessional poetry of modern American women virtually began with their reconsideration of the issue of incest. Anne Sexton and Sylvia Plath, like many of their successors, chose to expand their self-knowledge through courses of psychotherapy and to seize the opportunity that the evolving mid-century poetic school of confessionalism offered them to speak in poetry of private, subjective, internal experience. Both women attempted to fight clear of the oppressive weight of the male poetic tradition and succeeded to some extent by exploring the incest theme. Some of their poems, notably many of Sexton's, read like precursors to the recovered memory confessions of women today.

Sexton and Plath, who both ended their lives by suicide several decades ago, are still generating headlines. In her widely reviewed book *The Silent Woman*, Janet Malcolm, well known in her own right for her writings on controversies in the profession of psychotherapy, reports on the vexed relationship between the biographers and readers of Sylvia Plath and the executors of her estate. Plath biographies have also received extensive attention in the popular press. And in July 1991, a biography of Anne Sexton was noted on the front page of the *New York Times* (Stanley 1991) because of two startling revelations: that Linda Gray Sexton, Anne's older daughter who authorized the biography, had recalled memories of sexual as well as emotional abuse by her mother; and that Dr. Martin T. Orne, Anne Sexton's long-term psychiatrist, had released audio tapes of their therapy sessions to the biographer, which included Anne's intermittent recollections of childhood sexual abuse by her father. Linda Gray Sexton has since published her own life story as daughter of the troubled poet, which has received widespread notice in the media as well. Sexton and Plath have become cultural symbols of the current recovered memory controversy and its paradoxical elements of control and revelation, truth and fantasy.

Such attention should redirect us to their writings, the focus of chapter 1. In their poetry, Sexton and Plath explore responses to incest that range along a continuum from compliance with father-figures (Eunice donning Mummy's sweater and skipping off to Daddy's bank) to alienation from them. Their two "Daddy" poems depict these polar alternatives. Anne Sexton, through her speaker Orphan Annie in "'Daddy' Warbucks," demonstrates the material rewards of cooperating with an affluent Daddy, to the extent that a lack of eyes, connoting vision and even selfhood (eye/I) is taken as a loss at first hardly noticeable. Sylvia Plath also reveals in her poem "Daddy" a union with the father who is both a vampire (as in the game Night Trap) that sucks her blood and a Nazi who tortures her and attacks her individuality. The tone and style of the poem and its ending, with the speaker celebrating the vampire-father's death, convey quite clearly the daughter's alienation from and violent rejection of the Daddy when his dominance is imposed by social and psychological circumstances. And yet the end of "Daddy" suggests the speaker's demise as well as her father's. Daddy and daughter are psychologically and socially too intertwined to be separated successfully. Plath does attempt to separate from the Daddy, unlike Sexton, but does not succeed. Later poets, most notably Adrienne Rich and Sharon Olds, do succeed in separating and even in achieving something of a reunion with a redefined father, not the demonic Daddy. But first the problem had to be identified and understood; this is the achievement of Sexton's and Plath's poetry.

The term "Daddy," which both Sexton and Plath use as the label for their symbol of patriarchal power, merits some thought in itself. "Daddy," like "Dad" or "Father," connotes status and entitlement on the part of the father. But "Daddy," as opposed to "Father," also connotes affection and need on the part of the daughter, in that she addresses him in the diminutive, as if hoping to please him with her familiar subservience and thus win the favor she is seeking or to tame him with this informal title. "Daddy" also, however, presupposes both recognition and entitlement in the daughter, who can address the father with this relatively familiar title. Thus, in this term we see the two conflicting aspects of the daughter's Oedipal dilemma (which can be embodied here in Eunice and the scantily clad women of Night Trap, but which will be further explored in chapter 2): her necessity of deferring to patriarchal authority, and her necessity of denying the fact that she is compelled to defer by her position in the patriarchal structure, in order not to see her position as victim. She resolves this paradox by learning to take her father's desires for her own, resulting in an extended infantile emotional relationship with her father and later his surrogates.

The daughter who is also a writer has a special Oedipal dilemma, in that writing and publication are acts of treachery in a patriarchy if the daughter writes of thoughts and feelings not authorized by the father. Anne Sexton and Sylvia Plath are caught in these dilemmas and compulsively act them out in their poetry, being alternately or even simultaneously submissive and defiant. The recovered memory phenomenon, on one level, may similarly be an attempt by daughters in a patriarchal society to be defiant, to speak out their own thoughts and feelings and escape the subordinate role of good daughter, by separating from Daddy and facing up to the social and emotional realities of the patriarchal father, as we will see Adrienne Rich does (chapter 3). Those who are recovering memories may be, in effect, reliving the difficult Oedipal crisis and trying to alter the outcome. Chapter 4 shows how Sharon Olds achieves an Oedipal revision in her poetry, coming to address her male parent with the more formal and dignified (for both father and daughter) title of "Father."

Poems by Sexton and Plath that reveal the hopeful or desperate response of compliance will be studied in chapter 1, with reference to the classical Greek heroine Electra. Although open incest is not part of the story of Electra, her extreme closeness to her father and hatred of her mother, which enforce her own ongoing subservience to both, have led some psychologists to label a father-fixation the "Electra complex." Both Sexton and Plath imagine an incestuous father who is powerful and seductive but also devouring; they depict their own self-victimization in their images of loved but negating fathers and daunted or demonic daughters. The poems of Adrienne Rich, many of which reveal alienation from the seductive father or his cultural representatives, will be studied in chapter 3, with reference to the ancient Greek poet Sappho. Sappho's name has become for us synonymous with a separatist lesbian challenge to the moral judgments of the established patriarchal culture. Rich similarly refuses to victimize herself, as she believes Plath and Sexton did, by complying or by pursuing in her poetry an incestuous relationship with any father-figure.

Many of the poems of Adrienne Rich function as an attempted exorcism of patriarchal values and expectations by abstracting the destructive father of Sexton and Plath onto the social level of the male institutions of patriarchal authority and then separating from them. Rich for a time detaches herself from and rebels against all father-figures, finding solace in enduring mothers. The result, as she realizes in her later poetry, is personal empowerment as a woman but also some distance from the wholeness of life and some loss of greater spiritual power. Chapter 4 examines the poetry of Sharon Olds, which evolves a self-image midway between the opposing positions that Electra and Sappho represent. This chapter refers to the story of Sophia, goddess of wisdom, in many apocryphal accounts coequal with the male Christian God. The more recent poetry of Olds moves away from original experiences of incest and alienation and toward a symbolic, if not actual, equalization of father and daughter through the creative power of poetic language. Olds returns to Sexton's and Plath's practice of imagining incest with the father, but she does so, at least in her later poems, for the purpose of empowering and not victimizing herself. She finds she can create an imagined relation with the father that adds his social powers to her own creative talents. Olds creates images of a woman's imaginative use of her father, forming a controlled and creative response to the affluent and powerful, but destructive and predatory, father imagined by Sexton and Plath, and even to some extent by Rich.

At the end of *The Elementary Structures of Kinship*, Claude Lévi-Strauss compares the way the incest prohibition restricts individual freedoms and desires to the way social uses of language narrow individual experience toward a collective monotony (to be further explored in chapter 2). It will be the final argument of this book that modern American women poets, on the contrary, are learning to use the creative language of poetry, especially what has been termed confessional poetry, to explore and assert the needs and desires of individuals who have typically been victimized or at least subordinated by their culture. Women's poetry achieves this liberation by breaking from socially approved themes into open explorations of the incest prohibition and its effects, positive and negative, on women. As long as the incest taboo is accepted psychologically, the father's power is unchallenged. Once incest can be imagined, which is the accomplishment of Sexton and Plath, the effects of incest can be dealt with—first through rebellion, as we see in Rich, then through a redefinition of father and daughter roles, as we see in Olds. Whereas Plath and Sexton finally silenced themselves after great bursts of emotional revelation, returning to the voicelessness of victimage, many of their modern successors have found great power for personal and social change in the creative language of poetry. Many contemporary poets are redefining the demon-daddy of earlier women's poetry as a beneficent and nurturing father-muse: the father who can and will inspire (inseminate) his poetic daughter with the realization and power (potency) of her own creative mission. The poets, as usual, are ahead of us.

The redefinition of the father imago through the act of imagining

incest in contemporary women's poetry may also offer another understanding of recovered memories. The work of these poets evolves
from the realization of woman's degraded self-image in patriarchy,
to rejection of that image and the people and institutions that per-
petuate it, and then to a creative use of the traditional father imago
to remake a more positive self-image for women. Moreover, the
poems of Sexton, Plath, Rich, and Olds show us that in the quest for
full self-realization, women must test limits, and that incest, as the
oldest and strongest taboo, must in particular be explored. Women
must walk up to that barrier, examine it carefully, and cross over
it—in imagination, as these women poets have done and as male
poets have traditionally done in relation to their maternal muses.
Only when women have experienced what is most absolutely denied
them can they know parts of themselves and possibilities for growth
otherwise suppressed behind masochistic social roles. Perhaps this is
what recovered memories are currently accomplishing. If there is
any disease in these recovered memories of incest, it is not in the act
of reviving images of incest but in interpreting them only literally.
The literal image of incest is as much a barrier to growth as the
taboo itself, since it provokes punitive social responses. The poetic
image of incest allows for a more private and unrestricted confrontation with the self, with its internalized limits and its possibilities for
expansion. The poetry that will be discussed in the following chapters plots this course.

1

Anne Sexton, Sylvia Plath, and the Allure of Incest

LITERARY CRITICISM HAS TRADITIONALLY ESTEEMED ELECTRA TO BE A heroic character, but psychoanalysis has used Electra, like Oedipus, another of Sophocles' heroic characters, as the symbolic embodiment of potentially serious psychological difficulties. The "Electra complex" has been used as a psychoanalytic term to identify a type of arrested development in an older female child or woman, in which the daughter adulates the father and scorns the mother. This not uncommon scenario can become a more serious complex if the older daughter regresses to a state of infantile dependency on the father; as Carl Jung puts it, "If the sexual libido were to get stuck in this form the . . . Electra conflict would lead to murder and incest" (1980, 4:154–55). To the contrary, Sigmund Freud mentions the Electra complex briefly toward the end of his life as an acceptable norm for women, not as problematic as the Oedipus complex for men:

> [I]n females we find that . . . it is their lack of a penis that forces them into their Oedipus complex. It does little harm to a woman if she remains in her feminine Oedipus attitude. (The term "Electra complex" has been proposed for it.) She will in that case choose her husband for his paternal characteristics and be ready to recognize his authority. Her longing to possess a penis, which is in fact unappeasable, may find satisfaction if she can succeed in completing her love for the organ by extending it to the bearer of the organ. (1957, 23:51)

Note that Freud does not suggest that a woman might "find satisfaction" by discovering a source of strength within herself, thereby rendering her dependency on the phallic power of the male unnecessary and creating the potential for an equal social relationship between female and male. Freud does not see this possibility because he disregards the symbolic status of the penis as phallus, as embodiment of male access to social power in a patriarchal society. Freud sees desire as focussing on actual anatomical differences and thus concludes that nothing can be done about the differences between men and women, physical or social. Electra must just accept her fate.

Over time, feminists have noted that Freud accepts a condition that is considered pathological for males as being normative for females. Whereas the male must resolve his Oedipus complex to negotiate the tricky power relationship with the fathers he must live with and then replace, the woman is expected to accept the failure to resolve her Electra complex in order to negotiate the equally, if not more, difficult power relationships with the father-figures of her society.

> It is clear that for a woman to be healthy she must "adjust" to and accept behavioral norms for her sex even though these kinds of behavior are generally regarded as less socially desirable [than male behavioral norms]. . . . Although the limited "ego resources," and unlimited "dependence," and fearfulness of most women is pitied, disliked, and "diagnosed," by society and its agent clinicians, any other kind of behavior is unacceptable in women. (Chesler 1972, 68–69)

Phyllis Chesler developed this analysis of women's psycho-social conditioning in the early 1970s, less than a decade after Sylvia Plath's death and just prior to Anne Sexton's. This ambiguous normative-pathological state, as we shall see, forms the social background to many poems by Sexton and Plath, against which they try to understand their identities as women and poets.

Otto Rank, in *The Incest Theme in Literature and Legend*, asserts an additional connection between neurosis and creativity in the "incest complex," arguing that incestuous desire, when frustrated by the strictures of society, under "especially favorable conditions," can lead to "achievements we admire as the highest creations of the human spirit" (1992, 570, 32). But Rank also acknowledges the unfavorable role of the woman in both the experience of incest and the sublimation of that impulse in creative output:

> Just as the man is the active partner in wooing and in procreation, so too the development of myths and religions, as well as artistic activity, is intended to gratify and justify male sexual fantasies. . . . Whereas the man (father) is able to live out his repressed incestuous impulses toward

his daughter in violent and satisfying fantasies, in the woman (daughter), for whom such a solution is not available, the repression of attraction to the father, objectionable in our culture, frequently leads to neurosis. (300–301)

A careful reading of the poetry of Sexton and Plath raises the question of whether it is really repressed sexual desire for the father, for his penis as Freud assumed, that leads to neurosis, or rather an incompletely repressed desire for the father's power to actualize himself in creative social acts, which the woman has traditionally been denied. It becomes clear that these female poets desire the father's creative potency, often symbolized in cultural terms by the phallus, and not the actual father in his physical, personal manifestation; in the poetry of these women the father is used as a symbol of his own social powers. Sexton's poetry seeks the father's power to protect and affirm her; much of Plath's poetry seeks the father's power to advance her ambitions, to accept her as an equal. In several poems Plath draws on the story of Electra to explore her own relationship with this potentially enabling father. In fact, the heroine of Sophocles' *Electra* shows the psychological dilemma of the modern woman to be of long standing. Electra, like Sexton and Plath, seeks from an external male agent, her brother or father, protection and affirmation, fulfillment of ambitions and recognition as an equal.

Surely Electra compares well with her mother, Clytemnestra, who has helped to murder Agamemnon, her first husband and Electra's revered father, and who connives with her new husband to maintain Electra in an enslaved condition. But the Chorus (of community women) and Electra's sister Chrysothemis (who has acceded to the unfortunate reality she lives in without condoning it) frequently remind Electra that she facilitates her own enslavement, for Electra's open hatred and defiance of her mother and stepfather fuel their oppression of her. But Electra continues to find solace only in the thought of her brother acting as her savior, and she fantasizes her own rescue from her cruel mother and stepfather so far as to wish for the return of her father from death to aid her. Sophocles' depiction of Electra's fantasies illustrates several modern psychological theories. Otto Rank has noted that the "rescue fantasy" is "significant in human sexual life" and also "plays an immense role in mythical and literary fantasy creations" (1992, 65). Susan Kavaler-Adler has more recently observed that "the internal father will persist as a demonic or bad object within the psyche of the developmentally arrested female. The antidote is then often sought in the form of an idealized male rescuer" (1993, 72). And Judith Lewis Herman has written of the incestuous daughter's yearning for her father to confer "honorary boy" status on her and thus raise her out of the subordinate fate of women in a patriarchal society (Herman and Hirschman 1982, 57).

When Orestes returns and murders Clytemnestra, however, Electra does not join him but rather runs away, with the excuse of watching for the return of her stepfather. In fact, she never lifts a hand to protect or release herself, as much as she complains throughout the play of her subjection. Her open intolerance of her conditions, combined with her failure to act to relieve herself of these conditions, creates a paradoxical situation that cannot be resolved except by the power of an outside agent, an idealized rescuer who affirms the value of the person he labors to rescue. Electra chooses not to resolve her unhappy situation, either by making the best of her fate, like Chrysothemis, or by acting to free herself, like Orestes; she in effect chooses to remain enslaved until a "champion," brother or father, rescues her: "As I wait forever for Orestes to come and put a stop to this, I perish in my misery" (Sophocles 1994, 243, 191–92).

Perhaps Electra needs the implicit moral affirmation of rescue, since her persistent fidelity to her father is tainted by the primary reason for his own murder—the fact that he sacrificed his daughter, Electra's sister Iphigenia, to the gods to obtain their assistance in war. Sophocles' Electra seems unconsciously troubled by her father's morally questionable behavior. Though she defends it as the work of the gods and not his choice (217), she sings this interesting lament at the beginning of the play: "I shall not cease from my dirges and miserable lamentations, . . . like the nightingale, slayer of her young, crying out loud and making loud proclamation to all before my father's doors" (177). In a real sense, Electra does deny life to any future offspring of her own by persisting in grief for her father and not proceeding with her own life. In not being able to separate herself from the memory of her father, she symbolically duplicates his crime of sacrificing offspring. In the light of her father's questionable morality and her own submission to it, her courage looks more like folly. Electra's ambivalent stand between moral courage and passive fantasy haunts the poetry of Anne Sexton and Sylvia Plath, who both also struggle with the allure of morally questionable poetic fathers. Indeed, one might ask of these poets what the Chorus asks Electra in Sophocles' play:

But you will never raise up your father from the lake of Hades, to which all must come, by weeping or by prayers! No, leaving moderation aside and plunging into grief irresistible you lament ever, to your ruin. In this there is no way of undoing evil; why are you set on misery? (179)

⁓

Anne Sexton was something of a poetic phenomenon in the 1960s and 1970s; even more than Sylvia Plath, Sexton was a challenger of poetic taboos. For this reason among others, Sexton's friend and fellow poet Maxine Kumin portrays Sexton as a progenitor of the modern female voice in poetry:

> Women poets in particular owe a debt to Anne Sexton, who broke new ground, shattered taboos, and endured a barrage of attacks along the way because of the flamboyance of her subject matter, which, twenty years later, seems far less daring. She wrote openly about menstruation, abortion, masturbation, incest, adultery, and drug addiction at a time when the proprieties embraced none of these as proper topics for poetry. . . . Anne delineated the problematic position of women—the neurotic reality of the time—though she was not able to cope in her own life with the personal trouble it created. (Kumin 1981, xxxiii–xxxiv)

Sexton and Plath became revolutionary poets at least in part because they wrote within the poetic movement of confessionalism. Stylistically, confessionalism speeded the acceptance of "free" or unstructured verse. Both Plath and Sexton began their careers writing highly structured and formally intoned poetry, Plath's very clearly in imitation of esteemed male predecessors, such as W. B. Yeats. But both women soon learned to allow the emotional content of the poem to produce the structure, rather than prearranging structure to direct the emotion. As Jacqueline Rose has pointed out, Plath's poetic form "can be called feminine to the precise degree that it flouts the rigidity (the masculinity) of the requisite forms of literary cohesion and control" (1991, 28).

However, confessionalism had an even greater impact on poetic themes, as the internal, emotional life of the poet became the grounds for poetry, in part replacing the previously dominant social-cultural arena. Again, this thematic change, like the stylistic change, favored women writers, for it opened up what is perhaps a more traditionally female realm of experience to poetry: "Men are generally more verbal about 'justice' and 'equality' when it applies to abstract or public, global issues (*their* reference sphere): they do not apply such concepts to their personal or family lives—women's reference sphere" (Chesler 1972, 294 n). Even more seriously, many feminists feel that traditional male-authored literature, in its abstract or absent sense of justice and equality in regards to women, does violence to a woman's psyche. What Christine Froula has said of the woman reader resounds all the more loudly for the woman writer, who must try somehow to fit herself into the masculine tradition:

> Metaphysically, the woman reader of a literary tradition that inscribes violence against women is an abused daughter. Like physical abuse, literary violence against women works to privilege the cultural father's voice and story over those of women, the cultural daughters, and indeed to silence women's voices. (1989, 121)

By contrast, Plath spoke with great excitement of the movement we now call confessionalism as an "intense breakthrough into very serious, very personal, emotional experience which I felt has been partly taboo," with particular reference to the poetry of Anne Sexton (1966, 167–68).

Both Sexton and Plath were also influenced by personal experience in psychotherapy. Plath received therapy following her suicide attempt during her college years and again early on in her marriage. Moreover, Plath was fairly well read in Freud and Jung. During her later course of therapy she read Freud's "Mourning and Melancholia" (Plath 1982, 280), and in 1959 she read Jung's *Symbols of Transformation* (Stevenson 1989, 163), which focuses on the symbolic value of incest (and will be discussed, along with some of Freud's work, in chapter 2). Sexton began writing poetry at the suggestion of her first psychiatrist, while recovering from a breakdown and suicide attempt after the birth of her second child (Middlebrook 1991, 45 ff.), and her first volume, *To Bedlam and Part Way Back*, won acclaim for its many poems on madness. Paradoxically, Plath's and Sexton's disturbed relations to social norms both freed them to speak of such tabooed topics and tied them to personas with great yearnings for the approval of authority figures. In their poetry, Sexton and Plath both challenge and court male authorities, never quite finding an inner authority to speak of their own experiences without an anxious glance toward the supervising paternal figures of society. Kumin says of this regressive tendency in Sexton's poetry,

> It would be simplistic to suggest that the Oedipal theme overrides all other considerations in Sexton's work, but a good case might be made

for viewing her poems in terms of their quest for a male authority figure to love and trust. . . . [I]n Sexton's poetry the reader can find the poet again and again identifying herself through her relationship with the male Other, whether in the person of a lover or . . . in the person of the patriarchal final arbiter. (1981, xxix–xxx)

Such a "quest" is like Electra's persistent waiting for her brother or father to rescue her, and reminiscent of Electra's remark to her brother: "your pleasure shall be mine also, since I got my delight from you and it is not my own" (Sophocles 1994, 295). Sexton's poetic persona, like Electra, often seeks affirmation of her own emotions and experiences in an idealized and externalized male authority.

Sexton's earliest poems cultivate the voice of a psychiatric patient, who is necessarily dependent on her doctor for certification of her sanity and for the fundamental needs and desires of all emotionally intimate relationships. The opening poem of Sexton's first volume is titled in address to her psychiatrist, "You, Doctor Martin" (1981, 3–4). Doctor Martin is a Daddy-god to the speaker, omniscient and "oracular," while the speaker and her fellow patients are "large children" who wear smocks, make moccasins, and are forbidden knives at dinner. This childishly dependent speaker has little choice but to love her doctor: "Of course, I love you; / you lean above the plastic sky, / god of our block." In "Music Swims Back to Me" (1981, 6–7), Sexton finds no directional signs within the mind or within the mental institution, and the speaker must ask, helplessly and deferentially, "Wait Mister. Which way is home?" The doctor and the man who knows the way are soon joined by a young girl's Electral memories of a time of unity with her idealized father in "The Bells":

> Father, do you remember?
> . . . .
> I remember the color of music
> and how forever
> all the trembling bells of you
> were mine. (1981, 7–8)

"The Bells" portrays an idealized emotional union, a symbolic marriage between father and daughter, much like the naive trust in the doctor that is necessary for the "recovery" and release of the psychiatric patient.

Lurking behind such trust and desire for union, however, is the suggestion of incest between the poet and her father-figures, which surfaces in a number of poetic references to apparent sexual contact: "even my father came with his white bone"; "my father arching his bone"; "Frog is my father's genitals"; "I have known a crib. I have known the tuck-in of a child / but inside my hair waits the night I was defiled" (Sexton 1981, 111, 159, 282, 333). Most disturbing is the long poem "The Death of the Fathers" (1981, 322–32), in which Sexton portrays childhood memories of intimate moments with her father along with her present dismay at a more recent assertion by one of her mother's old friends that *he* is her real, biological, father. This confusion of fathers is partly based on events in Sexton's life (Middlebrook 1991, 342 ff.). In the poem, however, Sexton's speaker apparently attempts to resolve the confusion and determine the identity of her "real" father through the right to incest. The incestuous connection between father and daughter is established early in the poem, in a memory from the speaker's nineteenth year, as a "serpent" presses against the daughter as she dances with her father. Later in the poem, Sexton uses this experience of sexualized intimacy with the father as a standard in evaluating the claims of the other man.

> Who was he, Father?
> What right, Father?
> To pick me up like Charlie McCarthy
> and place me on his lap?
> . . . .
> and his tongue, my God, his tongue,
> like a red worm and when he kissed
> it crawled right in.
> . . . .
> dragging me up and pushing me down
> when it was you, Father,
> who had the right
> and ought.
> . . . . .
> He was a stranger, Father.
> Oh, God,
> he was a stranger,
> was he not?

It is tempting to read this poem through the object relations theory of the child's internalized good and bad fathers: "the preoedipal

female embraces the malevolent form of the father [demon-lover]—
which she cannot avoid doing, for he comes in tandem with the idealized father [muse] from whom she seeks rescue" (Kavaler-Adler
1993, 74). In "The Death of the Fathers," Sexton's speaker seeks
rescue from the intrusive father-pretender in the form of paternal
affirmation from the man she has always accepted as her father. But
even within such a psychological framework, it would not be easy to
establish that one "father" is the idealized muse and the other a
demonic predator because of Sexton's use of the right to incest as
her standard of evaluation. Can the ideal muse be an incestuous
father? The father-pretender's behavior is presented in the poem as
horrifying only because it is more direct and because the child did
not believe he was her father, not because of the nature of the behavior itself, in which the "real" father also participates, though
more subtly. The daughter-speaker seems to accept the right to sexual intimacies in the father she has always lived with but not in the
man who claims to be her biological father. It is as if she decides the
issue of fatherhood on the basis of the long-term emotional incest
of the adult man and young daughter who have grown together in
the same home. To this speaker, fatherhood is predicated on a history of emotional incest; biological fatherhood, like overt sexual
contact, does not qualify one as a father. Being a daughter, Sexton
seems to say, is not a physical state of connection but a complex
emotional experience in relation to the father.

With such poems as "The Death of the Fathers," Sexton's readers
must keep in mind her own depictions of the poet's or the sensitive
child's somatic experiences of another person's feelings or unreal-
ized intentions, as she has developed them in "The Death Baby"
(discussed in the preface). Sexton is always working more with emotions than with facts, and many of her poems emphasize the impossi-
bility of separating emotional experience from historical
experience. In "Mother and Jack and the Rain" (1981, 109–11),
Sexton suggests that a daughter's normal identification with her
mother leads her almost inevitably and naturally to a kind of vicari-
ous incest with her father: "On my damp summer bed I cradled my
salty knees / and heard father kiss me through the wall / and heard
mother's heart pump like the tides." Two later lines from this poem
recall vividly the frustrations of Electra in her subservience to her
parents: "I made no voyages, I owned no passport. / I was the
daughter." And in "Cripples and Other Stories" (1981, 160–63),
the speaker addresses another "father-doctor," calls herself (though

thirty-six years old) a "child-woman," and speaks of physical affection between the two of them. But the final two lines again suggest the symbolic nature of the relationship, as the father-doctor is
addressed in this manner: "I'm getting born again, Adam, / as you
prod me with your rib." The allusions to the stories of Electra and
Eve in these poems raise the connotations of the incest imagery
above personal experience and into archetypal knowledge. Jungian
psychologist Marian Woodman thus writes of the symbolic incestuous tie between a father and creative daughter as a spiritual, not
physical, marriage:

> For [the creative woman], the imagination is the real world, and the
> father-man who can penetrate and impregnate that world brings "light
> to the sun and music to the wind." He is her beloved. Here is where her
> intimate intercourse is. Here is where incest is permitted. (1985, 48)

The transference of this confusion of love and power in the Electral daughter's relations with her father to other father-figures in positions of social power is a movement of abstraction and
generalization that is often better captured in symbols than in histories of actual experience. Anne Sexton reminds us of this in a late,
untitled poem about a dream of a "My Lai soldier" who aims his
penis at her and says, "*Don't take this personally*" and "*It's my job*"
(1981, 575). Certainly this is a poem about the power relations between men and women (and their children) in a society that prefers
the dominance of masculine, aggressive power over the relatively
passive and caring natures of women; and the last line is certainly
ironic, in that the impersonality of the soldier's intentions allows for
atrocity. But Sexton is careful to introduce this vision as a dream
and to conclude it with what might be, a bit out of context, a sound
psychological warning—"Don't take this personally." Joseph Campbell has similarly warned, concerning psychic experiences of powerful archetypes, that it is important not to confuse such universal
experience with one's personal being (1973, 234)—in effect, to stay
deflated rather than risk inflation (and perhaps explosion) by archetypes much more powerful than the self. Sexton is, at least in
part, depicting father-daughter incest as an archetype, though she
often presents it in immediate and apparently personal terms. Her
speaker is acting out a part within this archetypal experience, and
so is the father-figure. As she has said, "Concrete examples give a
verisimilitude. . . . There is a lot of unconscious truth in a poem. In

some ways, as you see me now, I am a lie. The crystal truth is in my poetry" (1985, 103).

Sexton's explorations of archetypal experience within the context of literary allusion help to ensure that the experience is clearly symbolic, universal—not personal. In the volume *Transformations,* Sexton develops modern reinterpretations of traditional fairy tales that all little girls know. The most emotionally intense of these poems is probably the last, "Briar Rose (Sleeping Beauty)" (1981, 290–94). (For an exhaustive coverage of critical response to incest in this poem, see Skorczewski 1996.) At first, Sexton presents an objective, revised version of the princess's experience:

> . . . Little doll child,
> come here to Papa.
> Sit on my knee.
>
> .   .   .   .   .   .
> Come be my snooky
> and I will give you a root.
>
> .   .   .   .
> [The prince] kissed Briar Rose
> and she woke up crying:
> Daddy! Daddy!
> Presto! She's out of prison!

Here Sexton is working with the good girl's easy transference of incestuous desires from father to husband—as long as she works within the patriarchal social structure, does not challenge it, and obediently replaces Daddy with husband, she is "free."

In the last stanza of the poem, however, Sexton personalizes Briar Rose's experience, as the speaker reports no longer from outside the story, ironically, but now from within it:

> Daddy?
> That's another kind of prison.
> It's not the prince at all,
> but my father
> drunkenly bent over my bed,
> circling the abyss like a shark,
> my father thick upon me
> like some sleeping jellyfish.
> What voyage this, little girl?
> This coming out of prison?
> God help—
> this life after death?

Sexton, speaking now in the first person, draws in what seems to be the speaker's personal experience to anchor the traditional fairy tale in modern realities. All the poems in *Transformations* are deeply ironic, if not cynical, for all challenge the "happily ever after" (as long as the woman complies) mentality of the past with the observations of a woman speaking from a higher level of awareness in the present. More to the point, the traditional tale of "Sleeping Beauty," like the others Sexton draws upon in this volume, conveys the idealistic expectations of young girls who have heard these stories from their parents. But the last stanza of Sexton's "Briar Rose," and her ironic reworking of the tale throughout the poem to present Briar Rose in an incestuous dilemma, convey the disillusionment of the adult woman who has discovered the world is very much different from what she first learned to expect in hearing those fairy tales. As Sexton suggests, it is the deceptively romantic socialization of little girls that is at fault.

We see another victim of romantic socialization in the poem " 'Daddy' Warbucks" (1981, 543–44), spoken by Sexton's version of the popular comic-strip character Little Orphan Annie. This poem satirizes one of the chief allures of incest—the economic reward for an incestuous compliance:

> What's missing is the eyeballs
> in each of us, but it doesn't matter
> because you've got the bucks, the bucks, the bucks.
> You let me touch them, fondle the green faces
> lick at their numbers and it lets you be
> my "Daddy!" "Daddy!"

"Daddy" Warbucks' money, which comes from exploiting a war-obsessed society, is available even to a fatherless daughter who knows how to play the game:

> And I was always brave, wasn't I?
> I never bled?
> I never saw a man expose himself.
> No. No.

But such blind compliance has its internal consequences, as Annie realizes when she confronts the compromise of her own better nature:

> But I died yesterday,
> "Daddy," I died,
> swallowing the Nazi-Jap-animal
> and it won't get out
> it keeps knocking at my eyes,
> my big orphan eyes,
> kicking! Until eyeballs pop out. . . .

The gain of Daddy's bucks is bought with the loss of personal integrity, symbolized in the loss of eyes, the knowing, conscious "I" of the self. Orphan Annie, compliant woman-child dependent on her "Daddy" for survival, becomes a blind cog in the war machine—perhaps wearing an embroidered sweater and pearls, like Eunice.

In light of these archetypal presentations of the incest motif through literary and cultural allusions, it seems clear that Sexton's apparently personal poems on incest are functioning at least partly in the realm of archetypal experience. "Flee on Your Donkey" (1981, 97–105) is an important poem in this regard, for it depicts Sexton's experience of recounting memories of sexual contact with her father to her first analyst (see Middlebrook 1991, 56 ff.). There is in this poem another father-doctor conflation of male authority figures. At issue is the question of the memories themselves, whether they are actual or created; thus, this poem anticipates many of the controversies now surrounding the current "plague" of recovered memories of incest among adult women in therapy.

> Years of hints
> strung out—a serialized case history—
> thirty-three years of the same dull incest
> that sustained us both.
> You, my bachelor analyst,
> who sat on Marlborough Street,
> sharing your office with your mother
>
> .   .   .   .
> were the new God. . . .

The speaker's desperate need for reassurance, approval, affection from a father-figure creates confusion here over the nature of this "case history." If compliance with her father did not work to secure his love and protection, she seems to suggest, then perhaps she can please the father-doctor-god by meeting his expectations, or what she expects of his expectations, and secure the affirmative relationship she craves. The actual historical events in her relationship with her father seem to be less important than the emotional means of her ongoing relations with him and with his social substitutes; she speaks of "thirty-three years" of incest. Incest imagery becomes a kind of transaction between daughter and father-doctor in the daughter's mind, and the hoped-for end of this transaction is an emotional union expressed in allusions to incest, not unlike the young girl's happy union with her father in "The Bells"—a happy-ever-after fairy tale.

Eventually (as we will see in the conclusion to this study), Sexton's father-fixation, her Electra complex, will lead her to seek a kind of incestuous relation with the ultimate father, God himself. Even in "Flee on Your Donkey," a relatively early poem, Sexton makes a transition from her symbolic emotional relationship with the doctor-god to an intimate and symbolic physical union with God, the Father:

> . . . Soon I will raise my face for a white flag,
> and when God enters the fort,
> I won't spit or gag on his finger.
> I will eat it like a white flower.

Sexton's speaker presents these images after she has left her doctor's office for a mental hospital. The imagery of raising a white flag suggests again, as Orphan Annie also finds, that the means of being "saved" for a woman in a patriarchal society is self-surrender to the more powerful father.

The attraction of the symbolically incestuous relations Sexton presents between her poetic persona and her father and psychiatrist may be clarified by reference to another modern woman's writings on this theme. In 1992, in the midst of the recovered memory "plague," previously unpublished sections of Anaïs Nin's diary were released under the title *Incest*. These journal entries tell the stories of Nin's sexual seduction of her own father, a case of actual incest, and her physically intimate relationships with her two analysts, Rene Allendy and Otto Rank, which might be termed displaced incest with father-surrogates. Nin writes with a self-conscious control of tone and sureness of message that suggest these journals are not the spontaneous recordings of experience but their creative rewrites. However, whether these accounts are historically accurate or not, what is of interest in *Incest* is the freedom and rightness Nin feels in pursuing incestuous relationships with her father and her analysts. Possibly these relationships affirm Nin's sense of femininity, in Phyllis Chesler's definition of the term as "dependence on a man." Chesler believes that women who have sex with their therapists have "committed a dramatic version of father-daughter incest" (1972, 128): "The *sine qua non* of 'feminine' identity in patriarchal society is the violation of the incest taboo, i.e., the initial and continued 'preference' for Daddy, followed by the approved falling in love with and/or marrying of powerful father figures" (138). Clearly, Nin finds the feminine self-affirmation in these relations that Sexton searches for in many of her poems, and Nin does so without the guilt or ethical conflicts which Sexton never escapes.

In her relations with important men, such as her analysts, Nin not only seeks affirmation but also ensures that she is inflated by it, into a grandiosity that many analysts might find quite alarming. She writes of her first analyst: "Allendy. And tonight I need him. I need his strength. He is my father, my god—all in one" (1992, 55). And she reliably secures this strength; she manages to be rescued, as Sexton is unable to do: "I feel tonight that I want to embrace *all experience*—that I can do so without danger, that I have been saved by Allendy" (7). Nin leads up to her account of seducing her father with this heroic rationalization: "Today I am preparing to liberate my Father of the pain and terror of life" (153). Certainly she seems to have transcended her self-image as victim of her father's desertion of the family when she was a child, but only to use him and desert him in turn. She "recovers," if that term can be used, by duplicating her father's error and not by transcending it—much like Electra. After her affair with her father, Nin turns to her next analyst for "absolution for my passion for my Father" (221), and so begins an intimate relationship with Otto Rank. Then she cannot resist asking herself, "Should I go to Jung and get another scalp? . . . Jung, too, would become human with me" (358).

Incest ends with an account of Nin's choice to abort a child quite late in the pregnancy. She reasons that real motherhood would divert her from her true calling of caring for the men who need her. After the abortion, Nin cleverly redefines the event: "This little girl . . . I reabsorbed into myself. It is to remain in me, a part of me. I gathered myself all together again" (382). Voluntary abortion becomes a more passive "reabsorption." A daughter who would, initially at least, demand more than she gave, could not compete with men who compensated an outwardly compliant Nin with the questionable gift of an inflated role. If one definition of incest is "hoarding" (as we will see in chapter 2), then Nin's "reabsorption" of her daughter is, essentially, the final act of incest in *Incest.* Through the abortion, she upholds the right to self-protection she has gained from her service to the important men of her society; she cannot see any separate identity in the daughter she aborts, and she ensures the continuation of her privileged role as the woman who initiates and benefits from incest with the father and the father-surrogates—the special woman who must inevitably subordinate even her daughter to that predominant specialness. The potential daughter-child is sacrificed to ensure the priority in Nin's life of the "fathers" to be treated as her children, in turn reaffirming Nin as the esteemed "mother" of those patriarchs.

Anaïs Nin's story illustrates quite clearly the psychological allures and dangers of incest, symbolic or actual. Both Sexton and Plath eventually step, like Nin, toward symbolically duplicating the psychological process of incest that has victimized them. However, that step leads not to their hoped-for salvations, as it seems to do for Nin, but to their downfalls (as will be seen in the Conclusion)—perhaps because of their greater ethical sensitivities, or at least because of their distaste for the kind of groveling compliance with male authorities that Nin displays. Joining the patriarchy by becoming one of the boys, or the idolized mother-lover, is not a viable option for most women, who seek only to be accepted as they are and to express themselves as individuals. Plath and Sexton spent much of their poetic careers exploring the real need to find acceptance in the patriarchal tradition that excluded them from power, and at times they seem to find, or at least to anticipate, some positive alternatives to Electra's or Nin's self-enslavement to men.

In "All My Pretty Ones" (1981, 49–51), a poem on the deaths of her parents, Anne Sexton attempts to realign her relationship with them, seeking to create a more realistic and controlled love among equals in place of the compliant love of a victimized daughter for her feared and idolized parents. Here she remarks to her dead father, while leafing through his photos and diary:

> Now I fold you down, my drunkard, my navigator,
> my first lost keeper, to love or look at later.
>
> . . . .

> Only in this hoarded span will love persevere.
> Whether you are pretty or not, I outlive you,
> bend down my strange face to yours and forgive you.

Those final two lines anticipate the equal acceptance Sharon Olds later extends toward her father, an acceptance based on a recognition of his mortality and thus his equality with her in at least that respect. Sexton seems to recognize here the equality that mortality enforces and to accept a separation, rather than an identification, between herself and her father—hers is a "strange," not a familiar, face. And she offers forgiveness, indeed achieves the state of being able to forgive her father for his sins against her, for his imperfections. But the worrisome words at the end of "All My Pretty Ones" are "keeper" and "hoarded." Even though Sexton achieves some peace and reconciliation with her father after his death in the very fact of her ability to outlive him, she also hoards her relationship with him, keeps it private and separate and special, and preserves her memory of him as her "first lost keeper." Perhaps for this reason, for failing to take the next step of accepting her own equality with all people, preserving instead a privileged, symbolically incestuous relationship with the memory of her father, Sexton, like Electra and Nin, fails to accept herself as she is on her own.

☞

Anne Sexton had the opportunity, like Adrienne Rich and Sharon Olds, to watch her father age and die, to gain some insight and empathy for him in the process, and to replace him as an adult. Sylvia Plath had no such opportunity. Plath's father died when she was eight, and he remains preserved in her poetry in the extremely idealized Electral images of an eight-year-old daughter. Enough of her life changed after her father's death that Plath spoke of a tangible separation between the time before her father died and the time after:

> And this is how it stiffens, my vision of that seaside childhood. My father died, we moved inland. Whereon those nine first years of my life sealed themselves off like a ship in a bottle—beautiful, inaccessible, obsolete, a fine, white flying myth. (1979, 26)

The story of Electra thus intersects with Plath's story in several respects. Plath realized this and did not shrink from developing some

of the similarities in her poetry, particularly in "Electra on Azalea
Path," the poem she wrote after her first visit to her father's grave,
as an adult. If Sexton often shocked her audiences with the subject
matter of her poetry and was less daring in her poetic negotiations
with male authorities, Sylvia Plath was usually less daring than Sexton in terms of subject matter but more willing to explore the extremes of human relationships. As Rose puts it, "Plath regularly
unsettles certainties of language, identity and sexuality, troubling
the forms of cohesion on which 'civilised' culture systematically and
often oppressively relies" (1991, xii).

"Electra on Azalea Path" (1981, 116–17) relates a small part of
Electra's story as parallel to that of Plath's speaker, who says of her
father's death, "The day you died I went into the dirt." For Electra,
this entombment was a humiliating enslavement; for Plath's speaker,
it was her denial of the reality of her father's death, a denial that
allowed her to maintain her childishly idealized image of her father:

> It was good for twenty years, that wintering—
> As if you had never existed, as if I came
> God-fathered into the world from my mother's belly.
> . . . .
> Small as a doll in my dress of innocence
> I lay dreaming your epic, image by image.

When Plath's speaker does awake as an adult to the reality of her
father's death, she has to negotiate the unresolved emotions of
childhood loss and guilt that have been denied and brewing for so
long.

> I brought my love to bear, and then you died.
> It was the gangrene ate you to the bone
> My mother said; you died like any man.
> How shall I age into that state of mind?
> I am the ghost of an infamous suicide,
> My own blue razor rusting in my throat.
> O pardon the one who knocks for pardon at
> Your gate, father—your hound-bitch, daughter, friend.
> It was my love that did us both to death.

Plath's use of the Electra story in this poem implies that, like Electra's murdered sister, an earlier self of Plath's speaker has died
("went into the dirt") along with the father—the younger self who

knew that beloved father and had to be denied along with the reality of the father's ordinary death. The self that remains is the ghost of the vibrant, love-empowered self who was killed off, but also the heir of her unresolved ideals. The poem thus ends with an uncomfortable truce: both father and early self have died, their deaths implicated in each other, and a near-dead successor survives. Plath's command of her dead father's image is clear here, like Electra's, but later poems show a progressive shift in power from daughter to father.

In earlier poems, Plath protects herself from the growing power of her dead father through the distance imposed by death. "All the Dead Dears" (1981, 70–71), a poem that explores the tenacity of the dead in the lives of the living, at first depicts a "daft father" drowned in a pond. Nevertheless, Plath's image of her dead father persists, becomes "deadlocked," "tak[es] root" in the living daughter, and a "daft father" becomes gradually more deadly in power, more demonic. For an ambitious daughter, who hopes to make her own mark in the realm of literature, the father's death represents a loss—the loss of the one male who might be positively enough disposed toward her to lend a hand in her ambitions, to lend her some of his social power to succeed in her desires. In essence, a dead father is as useless, or as powerful in opposition, as an enemy; the result of his abandonment is loss and disappointment of personal hopes.

> My father died, and when he died
> He willed his books and shell away.
> The books burned up, sea took the shell,
> But I, I keep the voices he
> Set in my ear, and in my eye
> The sight of those blue, unseen waves. . . .
> ("On the Decline of Oracles," Plath 1981, 78)

A dead father does not assist his living daughter, as even Electra found; to the contrary, his memory is served by her life. Plath's speaker is dispossessed of her father's tools of creative power, though she clings to his words and visions. She tries to carry on his mission without his power.

Eventually, the Electral daughter loses sight of her own ambitions and desires in her preoccupation with her dead father, and he becomes a demon-lover—an all-powerful loved one demanding full, selfless attention and service from the daughter. (The demon-lover

is discussed further in Chapter 2.) In a very early poem, "On Looking into the Eyes of a Demon Lover" (1981, 325), Plath's persona
seems to feel dangerously immune to the power of the demon lover,
as if she were so unfortunate to begin with that he would take pity
and reverse her haggard self to love and beauty. But later, more mature poems show a gradual but sure growth in the dead father's seductive and selfish power. It is as if without a father to help advance
her own personal goals, the daughter is depleted of will and power
and must live for him, perhaps also hoping that a union with him in
death would result, paradoxically, in an empowerment of herself. In
"Full Fathom Five" (1981, 92–93), the father-figure, an old god of
the sea, already assumes some of the colossal and dangerous proportions of later, more full-blown manifestations. He is only partly
known on the surface of the sea, or consciousness, and what is not
known below is dangerous.

> . . . You defy other godhood.
> I walk dry on your kingdom's border
> Exiled to no good.
>
> Your shelled bed I remember.
> Father, this thick air is murderous.
> I would breathe water.

The attraction of a union with the father is the empowerment that
an orphaned daughter lacks. But if the speaker were to join her
father in his ocean-home, she would lose her selfhood as surely as
Sexton's Orphan Annie loses her eyes in complying with "Daddy"
Warbucks to secure her survival.

"Full Fathom Five" is a more sober version of Sexton's " 'Daddy'
Warbucks." In both poems, the daughter seeks union with the powerful father. Plath's recognition in this poem of the father's dual nature, both demonic and redemptive, illustrates Kavaler-Adler's
description of how a woman moves through psychic cycles

> of projecting the demonic part object outward in an attempt to rid her-
> self . . . of distress provoked by terror over the bad object's power to
> annihilate, destroy, or injure the self, while also seeking fantasy union
> with the idealized part object for self-protection. (1993, 41)

As the poem shows, however, such protection and consummation
are won only through death, never in this world of life. In "The Bee-

keeper's Daughter" (1981, 118), amidst a world of natural fertility, the speaker's heart is kept under her father's foot. Like the queen bee, though unrivalled even by a mother and served by male drones and by the "Father, bridegroom," she must be sequestered in her hive, segregated from life: "The queen bee marries the winter of your [father's] year." Kavaler-Adler explains why the idealized father turns evil:

> Inevitably, an idealized god turns malicious and malignant, for in the state of desire, when merger is sought there is the threat of self-loss that comes with the desired merger. This "bad" object now is felt to be intruding through strangling or to be devouring through some form of primal erotic swallowing and rape. It can also be felt as suffocating, or as abandoning by means of coldness, remoteness, and indifference. (71)

Notably, the paternal god of these poems is addressed with the formal "Father," not the familiar "Daddy"—he is still a frightening and not yet familiar being. The daughter remains distant from and reverent towards her idolized father.

"The Colossus" (1981, 129–30) again draws on the story of Electra, with reference to the *Oresteia*. In this poem, Plath's speaker has managed to raise the remains of her father out of the water—to bring memory-images of him up to consciousness, in effect. But, no longer buoyed by that other element, the father has broken apart into immovable pieces, much larger than life. His great size and power, however, fail to benefit the speaker:

> Perhaps you consider yourself an oracle,
> Mouthpiece of the dead, or of some god or other.
> Thirty years now I have labored
> To dredge the silt from your throat.
> I am none the wiser.

The daughter tends to him subserviently, labors to clean and reassemble his parts, but in the process she loses her own life and fails to revive his.

> The sun rises under the pillar of your tongue.
> My hours are married to shadow.
> No longer do I listen for the scrape of a keel
> On the blank stones of the landing.

This is an Electral daughter so closely bound to her dead father that she never departs from her intimate relationship with his remains and is no longer aware of any other possibilities for her own life in the world beyond. In effect, she has surrendered the world of reality and committed herself to the realm of fantasy.

Kavaler-Adler remarks on such an idealized father assuming an "archaic, grandiose form": "interactions with the father are intra-psychically experienced as sadomasochistic in nature, since grandiose objects impinge rather than engage in dialogue" (36). Plath's speaker is, literally, "married to shadow," at a dead end herself. A slightly later poem, titled "A Life" (1981, 149–50), depicts a female figure inside a glass dome, aging in the trap of her own life, frozen in a similar relationship with a drowned man who crawls up out of the sea toward her. "Good" behavior may court the gratification of personal desires in Plath's poetry, but it always ends up gratifying the father-figure, the powerful male other, and even inviting an attack. Even through the daughter's denial, even in old age, even after his death, he insists on asserting his presence in her life. In "Stopped Dead" (1981, 320), the speaker seems to bargain with another father-figure, not unlike Sexton's "Daddy" Warbucks (the tone also anticipates Sexton's poem). The speaker's compliance takes the form of going along for a ride in a rich uncle's car. But this speaker, like Sexton's Orphan Annie, finds that a loss of self is the end of compliance; the ride ends at the edge of a cliff. The speaker has the choice of clinging to the rich uncle for safety or of getting out of the car and facing a life without foundation in society.

The speaker of "Fever 103°" (1981, 231–32) seeks more defiantly and proudly to purge herself of her whorish, compliant selves. Interestingly, these selves she casts off are referred to as "old whore petticoats," and they are associated with the repetition of masculine pronouns, as if the compliant female is not really a woman but what Herman has called "an honorary boy" (Herman and Hirschman 1982, 57). Again, this process of purgation and purification is greatly desired but also unavoidably delusional and self-destructive, like the experience of a high fever. And the controlled alternative, as presented in another poem, is equally distressing:

> I am his.
> Even in his
>
> Absence, I
> Revolve in my
> Sheath of impossibles. . . .
>
> ("Purdah," Plath 1981, 243)

Plath's persona is nearly always caught between the ambitions that lead her to seek union with the father-figure and the degradation she must suffer in trying to fulfill them, a paradox quite similar to Electra's condition. Eventually, Plath's persona is driven to a kind of madness, to a frenzied parody of her poorly fitting social role, to a defiant exhibitionism running on the conflicted energies of self-hatred and pride. Jacqueline Rose has written of some of the results of frustrated ambition in Plath's writing:

> For if we have come to acknowledge that writing may involve for the woman an enforced male identification, condition of entry for women into a tradition which has only partially allowed them a place, we have perhaps asked ourselves less what type of strange, perverse, semi-licensed pleasures such an identification might release. In this instance, that license, that pleasure, shows the woman rediscovering herself as pure stereotype, as the reduced, reified and fragmented bits and pieces of sex. (1991, 117)

In "Lady Lazarus" (1981, 244–47), the potentially salutary peeling-off of corrupt social selves becomes the more terrifying and degrading peeling away of lives; attempted suicide becomes a striptease designed to titillate the audience that demands compliance from a talented woman unable to develop her skills socially. Where Nin learns to enjoy her own performance because she regards it from the viewpoint of her gratified paternal heroes, Plath suffers the humiliating irony of watching her own degradation in the conflict between her subjective, emotional point of view and the expectations of society.

> . . . Dying
> Is an art, like everything else.
> I do it exceptionally well.
>
> I do it so it feels like hell.
> I do it so it feels real.
> I guess you could say I've a call.
> . . . .
> There is a charge
>
> For the eyeing of my scars, there is a charge
> For the hearing of my heart—
> It really goes. . . .

The society that requires the death of a woman's internal, subjective sense of self in the attempt to gain personal desires, the society that creates this paradox, must enjoy the spectacle of this writhing, exhibitionistic, masturbatory self-torture—a sustained suicide of soul that never ends, since it leaves the body intact. All the frenzied speaker can do is magnify her powers of suffering beyond the punitive powers of her tormentors, who are already themselves magnified beyond the father to the most powerful of patriarchal figures. The result is a potent, predatory self that conquers the enemy by adopting his own practices and then turning them back upon him.

> . . . So, so Herr Doktor.
> So, Herr Enemy.
>
> I am your opus,
> I am your valuable,
> The pure gold baby
>
> That melts to a shriek.
> I turn and burn.
> Do not think I underestimate your great concern.
>
> . . . .
> Herr God, Herr Lucifer
> Beware
> Beware.
>
> Out of the ash
> I rise with my red hair
> And I eat men like air.

This ending of "Lady Lazarus," which many critics have preferred to read as the strong and affirmative voice of an independent woman, actually shows the speaker's ultimate entrapment. Playing the violent, male part of the patriarchal game, rather than the submissive role usually played by the woman, is not an escape from the limitations of patriarchy. The violence that is committed is just as damaging to the woman's self as the violence that is endured. In reference to the ending of "Lady Lazarus," Rose speaks of the "risk that feminism might find itself reproducing the form of phallocentrism at the very moment when it claims to have detached itself most fully from patriarchal power" (1991, 149). Both Plath and Sexton saw some of the advantages of compliance; they had desires and needs that they believed could be met through their compliance with patriarchal figures. But they both found that the sacrifices entailed were greater than the gains; they both found passive compliance finally unendurable, a point I will return to in the conclusion. Plath and Sexton stated the dilemma of all ambitious and aware women in a patriarchal society, but they failed to find a solution. They became locked in confrontation with the very father-figures from whom they sought relief, satisfaction, and acceptance. Rose speaks of victimization as a "pull" as much as a "predicament" (232), and in her discussion of Plath's "The Rabbit Catcher," she comments on Plath's exploration of both experiences:

> The poem seems remarkable for the way it can offer this political analysis of patriarchal power (violence against nature, violence of the Church, and in the home) at the same time as representing, in terms of sexual pleasure and participation, the competing strains of women's relationship to it. . . . Thus Plath sits on the edge of two contrary analyses of women's relationship to patriarchal power. (141)

Some light may be shed on this dilemma by Twitchell's discussion of the vampire novel as a type of "female *Bildungsroman*," in that the woman must fight off the seduction of a demon-lover. If he is to succeed, the vampire must first persuade the woman to remove her crucifix, since he cannot transgress that greater spiritual power. As Twitchell notes, this is an effort to have the woman "renounce a more powerful Father" (1987, 71), a symbolic father with even greater power than the demon-lover physically before her. Whether the woman yields to the immediate sexual pull of the demon-lover or puts her faith in the symbolic Father is key to the survival of the woman, psychologically: whether she will survive in her own right or be seduced into reproducing the activities of her demon-lover. Chapter 4 will demonstrate that the choice of a symbolic Father over the incestuous Daddy is what allows Sharon Olds to avoid the trap into which Plath and Sexton fall.

One must wonder where Plath's great talents might have led her had she heeded the warning and response preserved in one of her earliest poems, "Bluebeard" (1981, 305):

> I am sending back the key
> that let me into bluebeard's study;
> because he would make love to me
> I am sending back the key;
> in his eye's darkroom I can see
> my X-rayed heart, dissected body. . . .

Such an evasive course might well have extended Plath's life, but it would not have endowed her heirs with a poetic statement of the dilemma that still needed a solution. What Adrienne Rich has said of Anne Sexton applies equally to Plath: the achievements of her poetry redeem the loss of her life. Both poets offered the grounds for a new beginning.

> I think of Anne Sexton as a sister whose work tells us what we have to fight, in ourselves and in the images patriarchy has held up to us. Her poetry is a guide to the ruins, from which we learn what women have lived and what we must refuse to live any longer. Her death is an arrest: in its moment we have all been held, momentarily, in the grip of a policeman who tells us we are guilty of being female, and powerless. But because of her work she is still a presence; and as Tillie Olsen has said: "Every woman who writes is a survivor." (Rich 1979, 122–23)

2

A Modern History of Incest,
from Inside Out

ANNE SEXTON'S "DADDY" WARBUCKS AND SYLVIA PLATH'S NAZI-VAMPIRE "Daddy" share the characteristic of power, not only over their daughters but over much of society as well. Plath and Sexton were intuitively right to conflate the father's personal power over the daughter with social power in the public realm in their Daddy figures. What the daughter experiences personally in relation to her Daddy is representative of the workings of a patriarchal society, in which certain men are privileged with power over other groups of people and are inflated by their identification with that power. In a patriarchal social system, women are the primary "other," against which men measure their power. If the father thus symbolizes power within a family group, the daughter embodies submission and powerlessness, being the one individual in that group who does not share the father's power—and will not, until she is "given" to another man, whose power she will then share in a limited way. The poetic insight of Sexton and Plath into the father imago holds true through virtually all scholarly studies of incest, whether psychological or sociological. The common element is the issue of power. Many male psychologists and sociologists have struggled, mostly unawares, with the dilemma thus developed: how to study the phenomenon of incest while taking into account male access to power, which the scholar himself enjoys. It would seem that an open confrontation with the issue of incest would bring the question of paternal power under the microscope first. But this has not been the case.

Since the experience of incest and the taboo against it both stand at the intersection of personal experience and social requirements, between private and public domains, both psychology and sociology deal with incest as a central issue. Sigmund Freud presents the most interesting case of a male scholar struggling with the issue of incest, in his changing attitudes toward the incest stories of his female patients. Freud's investigations led him from an initial simple identification of actual incest as the cause of the psychological disorder then called hysteria to later theories on the Oedipal complex, fantasy, and wish-fulfillment. This turnaround, which still has repercussions in the psychiatric profession today, contributed to the break between Freud and C. G. Jung at the inception of psychoanalysis as a profession. Jung (1965, 167) agreed with Freud's later judgment that most incest accounts reported in analysis were fantasies rather than actual experiences, but Jung differed from Freud in two important respects. Jung did not denigrate these fantasies as unreal because they were not based in physical experience, nor did he interpret them as signs of a woman's natural subordination to the fathers of society. Jung rather saw these "fantasies" as vehicles for psychological maturation and spiritual growth—what he called individuation. Thus, at the very beginning of psychoanalysis, the issue of incest imagery opened up two avenues of development: as a judgmental, limiting, socializing experience for women in a patriarchal society, in effect putting them in their proper place; and as an enlarging, spiritual process of breaking a state of codependency with the parents and finding a higher spiritual identity. This bifurcation of opinions is remarkably like the divided responses to recovered memory syndrome today: that it is a kind of evil possession or "plague," to be wiped out as quickly and thoroughly as possible by rational means; or that it is an avenue for greater consciousness in women confronting their reality and questioning their position in a patriarchal society.

Still, the issue of power holds the discordant theories of Freud and Jung together. Whether incest is a woman's fantasized means of attaining social power as symbolized in her desire for her father's penis (Freud's sense of it), or her psychological attempt to transcend the limitations of her father's power over her (Jung's sense of it), or even the reality of sexual abuse that both analysts downplayed, it is the father's access to power that the woman lusts for, seeks to transcend, or suffers from. Similarly, many sociologists have studied the origins of the incest taboo in an attempt to identify the transition of humankind from animal existence to the more enlightened state of culture. Again, these studies agree on the central element of power. Two of the most interesting are Emile Durkheim's analysis of the incest taboo as a cultural defense developed to control the frightening power of the supernatural as it manifested itself in the blood of women and Claude Lévi-Strauss's study of the incest taboo as a means of sharing the most valuable of social goods—women—in order to enforce the experiences of community and cooperation and avoid social disintegration through interfamilial conflicts. In both cases, men benefit from the incest taboo by gaining the power to manipulate women. As in Jung's break with Freud, however, Durkheim differs from Lévi-Strauss in attributing some positive potential to women in the confrontation with incest or the incest taboo.

Remarkably, in none of these studies (with the sole exception of Freud's original, rejected understanding of hysteria) is the *woman*'s experience of incest and the incest taboo, whether social or emotional or physical, considered. Incest and its prohibition are explored as predominantly male experiences by these male scholars. Lévi-Strauss makes one weak attempt to reassure his female readers that he is not insensitive to their feelings:

> The female reader, who may be shocked to see womankind treated as a commodity subjected to transactions between male operators, can easily find comfort in the assurance that the rules of the game would remain unchanged would it be decided to consider the men as being exchanged by women's groups. (1956, 284)

The probability that women might not easily find comfort in such a "game," whose players' positions are unlikely to be changed without major social upheavals, or that many women might not even wish to play such power games at all, may be lost on Lévi-Strauss and many of his colleagues in the fields of sociology and psychology. But that frustration is at the heart of many of the best poems by modern American women poets, who witness to the emotional experiences of this most valuable social commodity. As anthropologist Gayle Rubin has noted, "it is the partners, not the presents, upon whom reciprocal exchange confers its quasi-mystical power of social linkage. The relations of such a system are such that women are in no position to realize the benefits of their own circulation" (1975, 174).

This chapter reviews some of the major theories on incest by Freud and Jung, Durkheim and Lévi-Strauss, in order to assess the intellectual underpinnings of patriarchy during the early and middle periods of this century: the intellectual ideas that justified the "game" women had to play or else subvert at their own risk, and thus the "game" that modern women poets have confronted. Both the Freud/Jung and the Durkheim/Lévi-Strauss pairings present

the alternative interpretations of incest as socially limiting or spiritually enabling. It is interesting to observe that decades before the current controversy over recovered memories, scientists were already
struggling to define the experience of incest and failing ultimately
to separate the social from the psychological components, the "reality" from the "fantasy." This ambiguity seems to be an inevitable
part of woman's experience in a patriarchal system. Within this context, the incest poems of Sexton, Plath, and their successors speak
more clearly as a complementary revelation of the feelings and experiences of the victims of both incest itself and the incest taboo—a
component of the experience of incest not considered by these
prominent male scholars.

It is almost impossible to write of Freud or his theories without
becoming mired in the many competing revisions of his thought.
Freud persists as a controversial figure within the psychiatric profession, as demonstrated in *Time*'s issue on the supposed breakdown of
the field of psychoanalysis by way of recovered memory syndrome
(see the discussion in the introduction). The development of
Freud's career is dramatic in its own right, and many critics, including feminists, point to certain episodes as evidence of Freud's own
unconscious self-deceptions, which have greatly affected our social
self-image. Perhaps the major controversy of Freud's career involved
a drastic change of heart concerning the nature of the sufferings of
his female patients. Both Jeffrey Moussaieff Masson and Judith Lewis
Herman have reexamined this turnaround in Freud's thought to explain in part society's ongoing willingness to tolerate (through denial) the domestic victimage of women, particularly in incest. If the
memories of childhood incest recovered in therapy are just fantasies
operating as wish-fulfillments in an unresolved Oedipal conflict, as
Freud came to believe about the great majority of his patients, then
society has no responsibility to investigate allegations of sexual abuse
within the family or to protect the victims, or even to question the
standard configuration of the family in a patriarchal society—or so
it can easily conclude. In such an atmosphere, remembering daughters can be seen as perpetrators rather than victims of abuse.

Both Masson and Herman retell the story of Freud's initial efforts
to identify the causes of the psychological condition of hysteria in
his female patients, as he presented them in a paper entitled "The

Aetiology of Hysteria." Herman, a feminist psychiatrist, calls the paper "a brilliant, compassionate, eloquently argued, closely reasoned document" (1992, 13). Masson, a black sheep expelled from the fold of Freudian apologists (Masson 1984; Malcolm 1984), calls it "an act of great courage" and describes Freud's later retraction of the beliefs presented in that essay as "a failure of courage" (Masson 1984, xix, xxi). Freud's initial findings led him to express considerable empathy with the women he saw as victims of sexual abuse. Such sympathetic statements as the following would be remarkable were it not for Freud's persistent and illogical use of the masculine pronoun in reference to the predominantly female sufferers of hysteria.

> All the singular conditions under which the ill-matched pair conduct their love-relations—on the one hand the adult, who cannot escape his share in the mutual dependence necessarily entailed by a sexual relationship, and who is yet armed with complete authority and the right to punish, and can exchange the one role for the other to the uninhibited satisfaction of his moods, and on the other hand the child, who in his helplessness is at the mercy of this arbitrary will [Masson translates this phrase "arbitrary use of power" (6)], who is prematurely aroused to every kind of sensibility and exposed to every sort of disappointment, and whose performance of the sexual activities assigned to him is often interrupted by his imperfect control of his natural needs—all these grotesque and yet tragic incongruities reveal themselves as stamped upon the later development of the individual and of his neurosis, in countless permanent effects. (Freud 1957, 3:215)

Later, in a letter to a colleague, Freud proposed "A new motto: What have they done to you, poor child" (qtd. in Masson 1984, 117).

However, the intensity of Freud's initial empathy for the female victims of sexual abuse was later countered by how absolutely he rejected his own original ideas and feelings. After initially bragging that his paper would establish him as "one of those who have 'disturbed the sleep of the world'" (1957, 14:21), Freud began to question the wisdom of that very act, feeling great discomfort and incredulity "that in every case the father, not excluding my own, had to be blamed as a pervert . . . though such a widespread extent of perversity towards children, is, after all, not very probable" (1957, 1:259). Freud leaves himself open to questions about Freud's own self-deceptions in this passage. Why the absolute nature of the statement "the father . . . had to be blamed as a pervert"? Why "in every case"? Why including Freud's own father? Why the doubt over the probability of widespread sexual abuse of children? It seems in this passage that the doctor doth protest too much.

Later writings also are phrased too absolutely for reasonableness: "... if[,] in the case of girls who produce such an event [seduction] in the story of their childhood[,] their father figures fairly regularly as the seducer, there can be no doubt either of the imaginary nature of the accusation or of the motive that has led to it" (Freud 1957, 16:370; commas added to clarify reading). Freud says openly here that any "girl" who identifies her father as an abuser is imagining the situation—as if it were impossible for fathers to abuse daughters. And in defining the daughter's "motive" in making such an accusation, Freud's exculpation of the father goes beyond what an ordinary reader would take to be a realistically nuanced picture of common family life:

> Since childhood masturbation is such a general occurrence and is at the same time so poorly remembered, it must have an equivalent in psychic life. And, in fact, it is found in fantasy encountered in most female patients—namely, that the father seduced her in childhood. . . . The grain of truth contained in this fantasy lies in the fact that the father, by way of his innocent caresses in earliest childhood, has actually awakened the little girl's sexuality. . . . It is these same affectionate fathers that are the ones who then endeavor to break the child of the habit of masturbation, of which they themselves had by that time become the unwitting cause. (qtd. in Masson 1984, 12)

Such a great disparity between the innocent affections of the father and the unconscious manipulative responses of the daughter is hard to reconcile; it projects the daughter as power player and the father as innocent victim.

Masson argues that Freud knowingly suppressed his own discoveries about the frequency of father-daughter incest in order to protect his own father or his own experience of fatherhood—in the sense of his own position as an ambitious member of his patriarchal society. While some of Masson's argument is overextended, his exposure of the story of Freud's treatment of Emma Eckstein during the time he came to renounce his own conclusions about incest is striking (Masson 1984, 55–106). It is a sorry and rather sordid tale of the irresponsible behavior of Freud and his friend Wilhelm Fliess toward Eckstein, and of Freud's subsequent self-excusing, self-deceiving behavior. Briefly, Freud referred Eckstein to Fliess for surgery on her

nose—surgery intended, ludicrously, to relieve an urge to mastur-
bate. Fliess neglected to remove some of the surgical packing, which
later festered and caused a series of major hemorrhages when the
packing was expelled or partially removed by other doctors. At first
Freud felt sympathy and apprehension for Eckstein, but this response was soon replaced by concern for his own reputation and
that of his friend. Finally, Freud concluded that Eckstein's persistent
and at times life-threatening hemorrhages were emotional in nature, subconsciously brought about to provoke Freud's sympathy.
Freud thus removed himself and Fliess from blame for professional
incompetence and malpractice by reassigning the responsibility for
Eckstein's grave illness to the woman herself, and the originating
physical cause was forgotten.

The parallels between this story and Freud's later public statements about the innocence of the father and the fantasies of the
daughter, not to mention Freud's own turnaround from belief in his
patients' stories of incest to theories about their fantasy lives—well,
they seem to speak for themselves. One interpretation of the
Eckstein episode is that Freud could not acknowledge his own abuse
of power, his own use of the patient as a guinea pig for the realization of his ambitions, so he converted the needed fantasy of his own
innocence into "reality" by converting Eckstein's reality into a "fantasy" of seduction, in the process reasserting his patriarchal power
and her victimage. Masson's presentation of the Eckstein case, in
conjunction with the reversal in Freud's theories about the origin of
hysteria, is convincing and more than a little horrifying. And the
horror is compounded by the fact that Eckstein came to accept her
doctor's diagnosis—the "good" daughter entrusted herself to the
greater wisdom and power of the revered doctor/father, much as
Sexton's persona does in her early poems.

Herman also discusses the apparent duplicity in Freud's professional turnabout. She cites instances in which Freud changed the
identity of the abuser when he published his accounts of various
cases—from the father to some other person, often a nursemaid
(Herman and Hirschman 1982, 9). She also clarifies nicely what she
sees as Freud's development of a masculine psychology after aban-
doning his original diagnosis of incest as the causative factor in hysteria:

Freud went on to elaborate the dominant psychology of modern times.
It is a psychology of men. . . . [T]he incestuous wishes of parents, and

their capacity for action, were all but forgotten. This does not matter very much in the case of boys, for, as it turned out, boys are rarely molested by their parents. It matters a great deal in the case of girls, who are the chief victims. (10)

Herman is interested in the emotional effects in women of such a masculine psychology, which ignores the reality of the young girl's dependency on the much more powerful father. In this regard, Herman counters Freud on the issue of the daughter's erotic attraction to her father by pointing to how the father may easily exploit such attraction—much, perhaps, as Freud turned Emma Eckstein's vulnerabilities into a cover-up of his own questionable behavior. Herman explicitly counters Freud's assertion that the daughter's erotic attraction to her father evolves from his care for her as an infant:

> Rather, it is a reaction to the girl's discovery that males are everywhere preferred to females. . . . She turns to her father in the hope that he will make her into an honorary boy. In her imagination, her father has the power to confer the emblem of maleness (penis or phallus) upon her. It is for this reason that she wishes to seduce or be seduced by him. By establishing a special and privileged relationship with her father, she seeks to be elevated into the superior company of men. . . . Even when the girl does give up her erotic attachment to her father, she is encouraged to persist in the fantasy that some other man, like her father, will some day take possession of her, raising her above the common lot of womankind. (Herman and Hirschman 1982, 57)

Herman here convincingly depicts the double-bind of the female in a patriarchal society. If she is to be successfully integrated into her society, she must not (and usually cannot) grow up and become independent and self-sufficient; she must, rather, transfer her father-dependencies onto her husband and other male mentors in society. This is Eunice (discussed in the introduction), the young woman who has achieved a "happy victory" (the Greek meaning of the name) by wearing her mother's sweater and working in her father's bank. If she were to rebel against this infantilizing role, the woman would not be able to integrate into her society in such an approved or profitable manner. The point is, "incest represents a common pattern of traditional female socialization carried to a pathological extreme" (Herman and Hirschman 1982, 125). From Herman's perspective, incest is inevitable in a patriarchal society—both its actual occurrence and its less obvious and more insidious psychological manifestations. This is so because incest, or the right to possess a younger, weaker, submissive female, whether wife or daughter, is the symbolic expectation of the male in a patriarchal society (Herman and Hirschman 1982, 56). Diana Russell has likewise found, in an extensive study of women's childhood incest experiences, that one result of the experience of incest is that "millions of American girls are being socialized into victim roles" (1986, 12). To eliminate the incestuous nature of society, Herman argues, the structure of society itself must by changed: mothers must have social power and status equal to fathers. Freud tried to reason about incest from his privileged position within the social structure of patriarchy and thus failed to see the role of that very position and that very structure in the perpetuation of incest. Freud's theory ultimately defended the system, not its victims.

Carl Jung was at first Freud's collaborator and heir apparent, but he later broke from Freud over their conflicting interpretations of incest. Whereas Freud abandoned his first belief in the pervasive reality of incest as the causative factor in hysteria and replaced this conviction with a theory of incest imagery as a fantasy developing from the power relations between men and women, Jung developed that concept of fantasy into a pathway to psychic wholeness—more on the order of a love union between the masculine and feminine elements within the individual self. Jung's writings offer a deeper analysis of the internal experience of incest, though they show little more concern than Freud's for women. Jung became concerned with how the individual confronts the images of incest that arise within him or her and then works with them to achieve individuation, or the full maturation of the individual into independence and spiritual self-realization. Jung, that is, believed that an honest self-analysis on the issue of incest can lead to the maturation that Herman regrets as lacking for most women in a patriarchal society.

Jung's theory of the subjective experience of incest is more difficult to follow than Freud's, but it has great relevance to the incest motif in the poetry of modern American women because it seeks to trace the transformation of the infantile self into a spiritual self through confrontation with the incest experience, which is what the poets studied in this book seek to do with their Daddy or Father figures. And for Jung, as for these women poets, the medium of this confrontation and conversion is symbolism—the medium of poetry as well as of the psyche in dreams and visions. Jung's *Symbols of Transformation* was written to effect and justify his break from Freud by focussing on the issue of incest. In this book, Jung seeks to show that Freud's initial investigations into incest revealed only a superficial layer of unconscious experience, what Jung calls the personal unconscious. It is this superficial layer of unconscious imagery that works to trap a woman in her subordinate role in a patriarchal society, because these images derive from her experience within that society. Jung hopes to demonstrate, on the other hand, that a deeper consideration of the incest issue opens the individual to the wisdom of the timeless collective unconscious and assists in her transformation to a higher, more spiritual level of identity, not bound by contemporary social definitions (Jung 1980, 5:420).

Carolyn Heilbrun has similarly pointed out that Freud's reading of the Greek legend of Oedipus, as the basis of his theory of the Oedipal complex, justifies a patriarchal attitude toward women but is far from being the only reading of the tale: "When Oedipus tears out his eyes rather than gaze on what he has done, he seems to accede in the patriarchal myth whereby father-murder and mother-marriage become symbolic not of renewal, but of all anti-paternal crime" (1982, 12). Jung, on the other hand, saw the potential for symbolic renewal:

> Incest symbolizes union with one's own being, it means individuation or becoming a self, and, because this is so vitally important, it exerts an unholy fascination—not, perhaps, as a crude reality, but certainly as a psychic process controlled by the unconscious. (Jung 1980, 16:218)

One might say that Jung converts incest memories even further into the realm of fantasy than Freud, but Jung does this to demonstrate that they derive from an archetypal human fantasy that can be used constructively by the individual. And Jung never questions the reality of psychic experience. Incest images in poetry are called up semi-intentionally by the poet to explore certain social or psychological relations, which is very different from the experience of physical incest inflicted by an outside agent; Jung likewise deals with the potential inherent in such imagery, which he accepts as just as "real" as physical experience.

According to Jung, incest images in a mature person result from a regression of libido (or desire) that comes about because of social frustrations. It is a kind of psychological running home to Mommy or Daddy when things go bad. Thus, where Freud analyzes the child's Oedipal complex as an inevitable and largely unconscious process, Jung considers the adult's incest imagery more as a quest generated by conflict, in which the adult child will either separate from her parents psychologically, and become her own person ready to assume her own life, or remain her parents' child.

> When the regressing libido is introverted for internal or external reasons it always reactivates the parental imagoes and thus apparently re-establishes the infantile relationship. But this relationship cannot be re-established, because the libido is an adult libido which is already bound to sexuality and inevitably imports an incompatible, incestuous character into the reactivated relationship to the parents. It is this sexual character that now gives rise to the incest symbolism. (Jung 1980, 5:204)

At this point, the individual can either respect the incest prohibition and repress her incestuous desires for a renewed union with her parents, or forge forward and try to find a creative solution to the symbolic dilemma of being forbidden access to the parent who holds the potential for rebirth.

A creative solution is a symbolic union, much as we see in poetic imagery, and not an actual, physical act of incest. Such a creative, symbolic union is the very means of self-transcendence and transformation. In this regard, Jung recalls advice from Jesus: "Do not think carnally, or you will be flesh, but think symbolically, and then you will be spirit" (Jung 1980, 5:226). This is what we see operating in the poetry of modern American women who are probing the incest experience symbolically: "The symbols act as *transformers,* their function being to convert libido from a 'lower' into a 'higher' form" (Jung 1980, 5:232). Since "the incest prohibition prevents the son [daughter] from symbolically reproducing him[/her] self through the mother [father?]," the final creative product of union with the parent must be "not man [woman] as such who has to be regenerated or born again as a renewed whole, but . . . the hero[ine] or god[dess] who rejuvenates him[/her]self" (Jung 1980, 5:255; the additions I have made in brackets to the quote above represent an effort to render it more clearly relevant to women as well as men. Jung, like Freud, tends to refer to clients, even when predominantly female, with masculine nouns and pronouns; as a rule, he describes the male experience.) The self-generating internal heroine/goddess or hero/god that is the ultimate attainment of the incest quest is not vulnerable to co-optation, compliance, or codependence. The woman who has developed her inner goddess is no longer psychically enslaved to the reductive Daddy imago, who represents the powers of society over her.

When Anaïs Nin says of one of her analyst-lovers, "He is my father, my god—all in one" (1992, 55), she is reducing the father and god imagoes to the physical presence of a particular individual, a process Jung would call regressive. And since that saving father is an external being, Nin seeks a sexual rather than spiritual union with him. Rather than moving from desire for a particular parent or parent-surrogate to symbolic, spiritual desire, Nin tries to invest the particular person, and by extension herself, with those higher qualities. Jung seeks to show that the redemptive direction is, to the contrary, from the particular loved person to the discovery of the Good Father or god within one's own psyche, and not in the external, material world, where it cannot exist. A lasting psychic union can occur, Jung believed, leading to the creation of the internal god/goddess image of self, whereas sexual union is always temporary and often disappointing. Part of the process of achieving an internal union with the good parental imago, however, is the necessity of first challenging the dreadful aspects of the parent, which rear up in resistance to the child's incest motivation. What Jung calls the Terrible Mother is fearsome precisely because she is the concrete manifestation of the parent's denial of the child's desire. More subtly, the "terrible" aspect of the parental imago will threaten the child by seeking to consume him or her—an ironic actualization of the incest motivation. The child who desires an incestuous union must learn to see that such a union requires loss of separate identity; in essence, it is a psychic experience of reabsorption into the mother, much as Nin describes her "reabsorption" of her daughter.

For the daughter seeking protection in a father imago, the dreadful aspect is the figure referred to in chapter 1 as the demon-lover, and perhaps symbolized best by the ocean god–father in Plath's "Full Fathom Five." The father imago turns evil because he threatens to consume his daughter through her very desire of seeking refuge in him rather than standing on her own. Thus, Plath's persona says to her ocean-father, "I would breathe water" (Plath 1981, 93), because he lures her into the ocean of death rather than moving into the world of the living to assist her. The daughter who confronts this Terrible Father or demon-lover must then reassess her quest— does she really want a literally consuming union with the father-imago? The struggle with the incest experience is an internal quest, believes Jung, and the individual who finds a solution, a symbolic means of union that avoids physical union (consumption) but achieves a spiritual union of separate elements within the self, attains a kind of divine transcendence.

> The psychic health of the adult individual, who in childhood was a mere particle revolving in a rotary system, demands that [s]he should him[/her]self become the centre of a new system. That such a step includes the solution, or at least some consideration, of the sexual problem is obvious enough, for unless this is done the unemployed libido will inevitably remain fixed in the unconscious endogamous relationship to the parents and will seriously hamper the individual's freedom. . . . Wherever [s]he may be, the unconscious will then recreate the infantile milieu by projecting his [her] complexes, thus reproducing all over again, and in defiance of his [her] vital interest, the same dependence and lack of freedom which formerly characterized his [her] relations with his [her] parents. His [her] destiny no longer lies in his [her] own hands. (Jung 1980, 5:414–15, brackets added)

Stylistically, *Symbols of Transformation* is a strange book, for it seeks to explain the descent of a young woman into psychosis by examining her dreams and creative writings and then commenting on her inability to benefit from the warnings and insights embodied in her own creative efforts. Yet the analytical and theoretical passages, such as the one above, are always written as if about the dilemma of a man. It is as if Jung, like Freud, cannot succeed in empathizing with the experience of a woman unless he can convert her, at least grammatically, into a man. This habit has the ultimate effect of ignoring or obscuring the differences between male and female experience; for instance, does the questing daughter need to confront the Terrible Mother or the Terrible Father or both in order to resolve her incest motive? For the son, the case seems more straightforward, in that he challenges the symbol of his heterosexual desire and his parent of physical origin simultaneously in one being, the mother. But for the daughter, these two challenges are usually symbolized in different people, at least consciously: sexual desire in the father and physical origin in the mother. Does the daughter have a double quest? Does she need to challenge the Terrible Father and then the Terrible Mother?

If we read the above passage with feminine pronouns replacing the masculine pronouns, or even if we take it as referring to human beings in general, regardless of sex, Jung shows a concern for the psychological maturation of the individual and an insight into the

means of attaining that maturation through a symbolic conquest of
the subjective incest experience. We may lament Jung's lack of sensi-
tivity to the heightened problems of women in this regard as being
akin to Freud's dismissal of their hysteria as rooted in fantasy and
to Lévi-Strauss's callous reassurance to his women readers that their
problems are all just arbitrary rules in a game. The very insensitivity
of these great theorists to the intensified situation of women in regard to the incest issue explains all the more why the exploration of
the role of incest in the lives of women has had to come ultimately
from women poets themselves, who could expose their own representative efforts to transcend the temptation to incest through a
symbolic leap into a more spiritual sense of self, without the preju-
diced and narrow vision of paternal commentary. Perhaps someday
a communal confrontation with the Terrible Mother will come
about in the poetry of women, but clearly in women's poetry of the
last few decades, as well as in more recent experiences of recovered
memories, the primary inhibiting and threatening parental imago
has been that of the father.

⌒

More recent followers of Freud and Jung have developed theories
that to some extent reconcile those of their two predecessors. Perhaps the most influential of contemporary psychoanalytic theorists
is Jacques Lacan, whose primary contribution has been, in effect, to
combine the more literal theory of Freud with the more symbolic
theory of Jung. Lacan has, for instance, shifted attention from the
penis in Freudian theory to the phallus, the symbol rather than the
physical attribute. Thus, Lacan discusses the father's role in the
child's Oedipal complex in these terms:

> The father appears in this game as the one who has the master trump
> and who knows it; in a word, he appears as the Symbolic father. . . . The
> Symbolic father—he who is ultimately capable of saying "I am who I
> am"—can only be imperfectly incarnate in the real father. . . . The real
> father takes over for the Symbolic father. This is why the real father has
> a decisive function in castration. (1968, 271)

(As we will see in the conclusion, the one holding the master trump
is almost exactly the image Anne Sexton uses for God, the Patriarch,
in one of her later poems.) Thus the personal father functions sym-

bolically, to enforce castration of the child's incestuous desires so that the child may move out of the family and pursue his or her desires with greater freedom of action and effect. Moreover, the power of the father is symbolized in the phallus, the primordial symbol of unrestricted growth and desire—the absolute desire of being against which no human can compete. Thus the phallus, while representing in itself the absolute principles of growth and desire, represents for all humans apprehending it the curtailment (or castration) or their own selfish desires, such as incestuous union, which do not serve the universal force of growth. The phallus of desire and growth thus becomes a "bar" to many individual desires, not unlike that universal symbol of prohibition that has become so prominent in urban life—the slash bisecting the more feminine form of the circle.

In fact, Lacan associates the primary symbol of castration with the mother, the female Other.

> It is at the level of the Other, in the place where castration manifests itself in the Other, it is in the mother—for both girls and boys—that what is called the castration complex is instituted. It is the desire of the Other, which is marked by the bar. (187–88)

Thus Lacan's theory reinforces the symbolism of sexism: the father can participate in the power of the Symbolic father because he has the penis/phallus, while the mother represents the Other, the one of castrated desire. It is hard to believe that both girls and boys would respond to this symbolic scenario equally. Jane Gallop summarizes some of the implications of Lacan's theory for feminist thought on sexual relations.

> Lacan's contribution to Freudian theory of sexual difference is to articulate the castration complex around the phallus, which is symbolic. . . . The phallus, unlike the penis, is lacking to any subject, male or female. The phallus symbolizing unmediated, full *jouissance* must be lacking for any subject to enter the symbolic order, that is to enter language, effective intersubjectivity. Human desire, according to Lacanian doctrine, is always mediated by signification. That is our human lot of castration. The ultimate Lacanian goal is for the subject "to assume his/her castration." (1982, 95–96)

In psychological terms of the relation between the individual and any absolute ideal, such as God, surely Lacan's argument holds true. "Effective intersubjectivity" certainly would be enhanced by the equality attained through the humility of everyone accepting subordination to the ideal, such as recognizing the phallus as symbol of absolute power and not a personal possession. But in terms of actual social relations, Lacan's theory seems rather naïve. As Rubin has pointed out, "the phallus also carries a meaning of the dominance of men over women, and it may be inferred that 'penis envy' is a recognition thereof. . . . We still live in a 'phallic' culture" (1975, 191).

Traditionally, males have carried the power of society, even as they have carried penises; as so often happens in the psyche, as in poetry, the concrete object comes to symbolize the abstract value. "The ultimate Lacanian goal" may be "to assume . . . castration," but how often will a privileged being voluntarily cut off his own social privileges? This is an act of humility on the part of males that women have called for ever since the Wife of Bath tore some pages from her husband's book on evil wives—and how much has changed in that time? Many feminists, like Adrienne Rich, won't wait patiently for that happy day when the rules of the "game" are spontaneously and altruistically changed by men to benefit women. It seems more likely that, without great change, women will continue to assume the castrated social position they have traditionally held and men will cling to their social privileges. In this light, Lacanian humility reads more like maintaining the status quo, stranding women in their painfully compromised social position. As Rubin has put it, when the daughter "discovers that 'castration' is a prerequisite to the father's love. . . . she therefore begins to desire 'castration,' and what had previously become a disaster becomes a wish" (1975, 197). The father, however, does not need to castrate himself to win his daughter's love; he can assume it or command it. Rubin is speaking metaphorically, not literally, but her presentation of the young girl's situation illustrates the inevitability of the woman's psychological castration in a traditionally patriarchal society. Thus Lynda Boose concludes, "In both Freudian and Lacanian theory, the psychosocial dynamics of the family resemble something akin to an all-determining game of who's-got-the-phallus. By these terms, the daughter is clearly the one person who *does not*" (1989, 21).

In order to ingratiate herself with the father, who has social power, the daughter must substitute his desires for her own; she later automatically extends this service to her husband and other influential men in her life. "From the standpoint of the system, the preferred female sexuality would be one which responded to the desires of others, rather than one which actively desired and sought a response" (Rubin 1975, 182). Rubin sees the Oedipal complex not as the daughter's discovery of her inevitable subordination within society (as Freud argued) but as a more intentional "apparatus for the production of sexual personality" (189)—specifically, in the female, the "masochistic" personality that renders her pliable to men. Rubin's feminist restatement of the experience of the Oedipus (or Electra) complex for women is based on readings of Freud, Lévi-Strauss, and others. It is a rather harrowing scenario. Rubin describes how children discover sexual differences and the incest taboo, noting that children of both sexes initially are denied sexual access to the mother, who is the father's property. The difference is that in time the boy can grow up and have sexual relations with another adult woman, thus preserving his original sexual orientation. He has the phallus, so he has the right to sexual relations with a woman. The girl, however, experiences the incest taboo as a ban on women as a whole. She must learn to reorient her erotic love away from the mother/female and toward the father/male, who can share the phallus with her and thus grant her any power she might have in society (Rubin 1975, 193–95).

Rubin's empathetic analysis of the no-win situation for the young girl discovering her social role in a patriarchal society (discovering her status as an object of male will and desire rather than a subject possessing her own) casts light on the situation of Freud's hysterical female patients and perhaps on those women recovering memories of incest today. Perhaps unconsciously the daughter never fully accepts the defeat of her desires and continues unconsciously to try to get the phallus (or power to realize those desires) from her father or father-figure, but with a negative aura of guilt that keeps the effort unconscious, since even that attempt is forbidden as incest. The woman must then envision what she deeply desires in terms of it being forced upon her—in effect, given to her without her openly avowing that she wants it. The result is an unconscious addiction to Daddy, a powerful combination of desire and resentment that cannot be resolved within the terms of the system. Rubin concludes: "it is certainly plausible to argue . . . that the creation of 'femininity' in women in the course of socialization is an act of psychic brutality, and that it leaves in women an immense resentment of the suppression to which they were subjected" (196).

Kavaler-Adler also helps to clarify the problem, left unclear in Jung's writings, of whether women must challenge the Terrible

Mother or the Terrible Father, or both, in the incest quest. If the mother herself is inadequate, Kavaler-Adler observes, the child during the Oedipal stage will turn to the father for the missing maternal contact and nurture, which becomes sexualized (1993, 34). Later in life, the daughter may discover, as Plath seems to do, that the father imago she carries is superhuman in nature because of this dual character; he is essentially both father and mother. This may explain in part why Plath's poetic father is so often associated with water, more traditionally a maternal symbol.

> As the object of both oral and oedipal desires, with cravings for maternal modes of tenderness intermingled with oedipal yearnings for romance and for genital penetration, the father becomes mammoth in his tantalizing power of attraction for the little girl . . . "daddy" becomes the colossus and the Gothic god-daddy, extending to divine as well as to demonic proportions. (Kavaler-Adler 1993, 68–69)

The older daughter's identity is so bound to this inflated god-demon inside her that she cannot separate from him, for her own inflated ego is dependent on its relation to him. But maintaining the link to the godly father requires maintaining the link to the demonic father as well, and the composite god-demon-father is ultimately greater and stronger than the woman's own ego (Kavaler-Adler 1993, 102).

In the quote above, Kavaler-Adler is referring in part to the case of Sylvia Plath, whom she describes as pathological. Jacqueline Rose points out that many feminists object to Plath being labeled pathological because they see "the representative nature of Plath's inner drama, the extent to which it focuses the inequities (the pathology) of a patriarchal world" (1991, 3). Plath clearly chose or was chosen to act out in her writing the pathological circumstances of women in the modern world—what Freud describes as the woman's non-necessity to resolve the Oedipal conflict, since her role in society is to remain in a psychically incestuous daughterly position in relation to men. Plath was ambitious enough in her own right not to be content with this role, and her poetry records much of the torment and many of the insights that come from trying to renegotiate the inadequate Oedipal resolution. There is no Good Father developed in Plath's poetry, as there is later in Sharon Olds's. Plath, like Anne Sexton, uncovers the problem of the Terrible Father and leaves it to others to find solutions other than being consumed by him. Rose suggests further that the compulsive attraction of Plath's life and poetry is that they deal with an ambivalence between contrary ways of perceiving inner and outer realities. Whether Plath is literally, personally pathological or working creatively with metaphors of social pathology, Rose suggests, is related to the argument of Freud and Jung (Rose 1991, 104). Plath is, thus, an especially instructive example of the nature of psychic and poetic incest imagery, for in her work that imagery certainly functions both personally and metaphorically, as we saw in Chapter 1 with her adaptation of the Electra story. Incest imagery is usually neither just literal nor just metaphorical but some combination of the two, since the woman herself is both an individual person with her own psychic contents and a social being carrying archetypal images in her unconscious mind. Neither Freud nor Jung tells the whole story alone.

The question of the mother's role in the daughter's negotiation of incest imagery needs to be addressed briefly. The mother is an important actor in a family's incest drama, as Herman and many others have pointed out, since the mother's compliance with patriarchal norms enables the victimization of her daughter. And, as Kavaler-Adler has discussed, the failure of the mother to nurture the daughter will intensify the daughter's incestuous dependence on the father. One might say the Terrible Mother is a precondition for the Terrible Father—and a precondition that is often present, since the mother is usually more deeply absorbed into the patriarchal system than her daughter. The mother often becomes the primary agent in socializing her daughter to play the role expected of her, and this action is made even more problematic in that the mother has "got the phallus," in the sense that she has sexual relations with the father and gains somewhat from her access to his power, both of which symbolic benefits the daughter lacks. The process of socialization may well be perceived by the daughter as an act of subordination even to and by the mother.

According to Chesler, this dilemma is especially problematic for the ambitious writer-daughter, who has more difficulties than the average woman in seeking and accepting nurture from her mother.

Sylvia Plath [and other women writers] want and need mother love—but not at the price of "uniqueness" or glory. They are probably as maddened by the absence of maternality in their lives as they would be by the demands it would eventually place upon their freedom. The combination of nurturance deprivation *and* restrictions upon their uniqueness or heroism is deadly. They cannot survive as just "women," and they are not allowed to survive as human or as creative beings. . . . Such madness is essentially an intense experience of female biological, sexual, and cultural castration, and a doomed search for potency. (1972, 30–31)

So the ambitious daughter turns to her father as a source of that potency and thus sets up a very troubled dependency on him that all too closely resembles the feminine subordination she is seeking to escape. However, the father often turns away from the appeal—at times to guard his own authority, at times in a well-intentioned but ironic effort to avoid what may be construed, by himself or others, as incestuous contact. The result is that the woman's potential for confronting the Terrible Father and achieving her own integrity centers on her coping with the experience of abandonment by the personal father or his social surrogates. From Marion Woodman's neo-Jungian perspective, a woman's successful completion of the incest quest depends on how well she can turn this loss into a creative experience of growth.

For many women born and raised in a patriarchal culture, initiation into mature womanhood occurs through abandonment, actual or psychological. It is the identity-confirming experience that frees them from the father. . . . the internal father, who in the soul-making process they sought to please, turns on them—or appears to—as soon as that father-image is projected onto a man, or they seek recognition and reward in those creative fields still largely dominated by men. (1985, 33)

⌒

As the theories of Freud and Jung demonstrate, the founders of modern psychology were concerned, in the end, not with the social sufferings of women living in an incestuous society but with the concept of incest as a psychic phenomenon. Where Freud came to believe that memories of incest in his female patients were fantasies that compensated for frustrated desires, Jung at least offered an alternate and more positive view of incest images as potential vehicles for individual psychic growth beyond the frustrating limitations of society. Through the theories of these two men and their successors, we see both negative and positive interpretations of the subjective incest experience. Yet both Freud and Jung acknowledge that it is the conflict between the individual's desires and the rules and expectations of society that brings about the internal incest motive.

There is thus an inevitable complementary relationship between psychology and sociology in understanding the incest experience. As Lévi-Strauss has put it,

> The prohibition of incest touches upon nature, i.e., upon biology or psychology, or both. But it is just as certain that in being a rule it is a social phenomenon, and belongs to the world of rules, hence to culture, and to sociology, whose study is culture. (1969, 24)

Sociologists have focussed on why the incest taboo is so necessary to human societies that it is a universal rule which seems to define the origin of human culture. From the sociological perspective, we gather a sense of the effects on women, not of incest, but of the incest taboo itself. These effects, like their corollaries in the field of psychoanalysis, also have their positive and negative interpretations. And again, as in psychoanalysis, the competing sociological interpretations of the incest prohibition agree on one principle—the issue of power.

The theory of incest developed by Emile Durkheim is notable for its advancement of some degree of sympathy for the position of women in a patriarchal society and for its recognition of some disadvantage to women, not only in the fact of incest itself but also, ironically, in the incest prohibition. Other sociologists like Lévi-Strauss denigrate Durkheim's theory as not well grounded in facts (Lévi-Strauss 1969, 20–23), but Durkheim's thought, like Jung's, has symbolic appeal—it allows for some positive potential for women in an otherwise punitive social situation. Durkheim argues that the incest prohibition came about as man's effort to control the supernatural power he saw to be invested in woman, particularly in her menstrual blood. Durkheim's analysis thus focuses on incest and the incest prohibition as reflections of the power structure of society. From such a perspective, the incest taboo may mark not so much the turn from animal to cultural organization (as Lévi-Strauss sees it) as the turn from matriarchy to patriarchy, understanding matriarchy as a phase in which man saw woman as bearing a "hidden doctrine": "The mystery is entrusted to the woman; it is she who safeguards it and administers it, and she who communicates it to men" (Bachofen 1973, 206).

Durkheim reviews the terribly isolating experiences that the pubescent girl and menstrual woman historically had to endure because of the social requirement that they seclude themselves from any contact with the environment, which might contaminate the clan: the sight or touch of men, food, water, earth, even air and sunlight. The source of potential contamination was the woman's menstrual blood, but paradoxically this was so because the blood was taken to be the vehicle of the clan's totem, the supernatural force of the clan itself: "the blood is a divine thing. When it runs out, the god is spilling over" (Durkheim 1963, 89). Originally, Durkheim believes, the woman benefited from this assumed association of her available blood with divinity—she was sequestered in acknowledgment of her awe-inspiring condition, her greater proximity to the divine.

> All blood is terrible and all sorts of taboos are instituted to prevent contact with it. . . . Thus the woman, in a rather chronic manner, is the theater of these bloody demonstrations. The feelings that the blood evokes are carried within her. . . . The woman is therefore, in an equally chronic way, taboo for the other members of the clan. A more or less conscious anxiety, a certain religious fear, cannot fail to be present in all the relations which her companions can have with her. . . . [O]f all parts of the female organism, the sexual is the part most severely restrained from any relationship. . . . Whoever violates this law finds himself in the same state as the murderer. He has entered into contact with blood whose terrible properties have passed into him; he has become a danger both for himself and for others. He has violated a taboo. (83, 85–86)

Like the internal Jungian goddess, the woman bearing the divine fluid is beyond social power games. Durkheim's conception of women in early cultures anticipates current interest among feminists in a goddess figure, often identified as Sophia (who will be discussed in chapter 4). Durkheim shows, however, that this awe-full state of women did not last, as the dangers inherent in contact with the supernatural rendered the woman herself dangerous (as again the concrete body comes to symbolize an abstract state). Thus, her separation from the clan became in time a sign of her danger, rather than a sign of her potential power, and so man transformed supernatural fear into sexual segregation. The awe-full degenerated into the awful.

Durkheim believes that fear of contact with the clan's supernatural totem by way of woman's blood brought about the rule that no man may have sexual contact with a woman from his own clan, or extended family. Different clans have different totems, so marriage and sexual relations with a woman from another clan or family would not carry the same danger and stigma as contact with a woman from one's own clan. From this theory Durkheim abstracts his sense of the composition of the family today, and why the incest prohibition is still in effect everywhere when such primitive beliefs in clan totems are no longer in conscious operation.

> Incestuous unions . . . are odious to us, if only by the fact that we find mingled therein something that it seems to us should be separated therefrom. The horror that it inspires in us is identical to that which is felt by the savage at the thought of a possible mixture between that which is taboo and that which is profane; and this horror is well founded. Between the conjugal functions and the kinship functions, *such as they are currently constituted,* there is in fact a real incompatibility, and as a result one cannot permit confusion of the two without causing the ruination of both. (100)

If, argues Durkheim, a selfish kind of romantic or sensual enjoyment should intrude into the family and disrupt the moral duties inherent in each family role, not only the structure of the family itself, but the ethical structure of all society, would decay. Herman would agree, but would add that the most likely intrusion of selfish satisfactions would take the form of the most powerful figure in the family, the father, indulging himself with the least powerful figure, his daughter. Durkheim, as sensitive as he is to the issue of the incest prohibition as a sequestering or segregation of women, and thus a detriment to their fullness of life, does not deal with such ongoing realities of love and power as Herman discusses.

However, Durkheim concludes his study by discussing the link between the incest prohibition and such cultural pursuits as poetry. Where Jung finds the necessity for a symbolic transformation of identity in a courageous confrontation of the subjective incest experience, Durkheim similarly finds that the symbolic, artistic activities of culture are one consequence of the social prohibition against incest—they carry the romantic sensuality that is properly displaced from the family. His discussion of this relationship, like Jung's, affords an additional insight into the poetic activities of many modern American women who have confronted the issue of incest in their poetry.

> Once the prejudices relating to blood had led man to forbid all union between relatives, the sexual feeling was obliged to find a milieu outside of the familial circle. . . . [T]he clan, which is to say the family, became

and remained the seat of morality. . . . [S]ensuality found itself in opposition to the familial morality. . . . It is thus that the ideas pertaining to the sexual life became rigorously linked with the development of art, of poetry, and to all the vague dreams and aspirations of the spirit and of the heart, to all the individual or collective manifestations where the imagination plays the largest part. (Durkheim 1963, 108–10)

As Rank (1992) and Twitchell (1987) convincingly demonstrate, art at any level is certainly not free of the incest motif. Art may carry the romantic sensuality that is displaced from the family, but it still often focusses on the temptation to indulge such desires within the family. The symbolic value of incest is clearly a vexed question that humankind has not yet fully resolved, and perhaps the failure to consider further the element of power in familial and social relationships explains in part Durkheim's rather rosy vision of art, as well as the return of the incest motif in the poetry of modern American women.

The positive aspect of Durkheim's theory, however, is that it acknowledges, as Lévi-Strauss's does not, an important social and spiritual power inherent in women themselves (and not just in the images men hold of them), which men have dreaded and tried to suppress by means of the incest taboo. This may help to explain why women poets have resumed the symbolic exploration of incest. If, according to Durkheim's theory, the prohibition against incest led to a disempowerment of women through social segregation and subordination, perhaps a new exploration of incest would lead to a new empowerment. Choosing the spiritual potential over the material debasement—envisioning women as vessels of spiritual power, as in Durkheim's theory, rather than as the prime commodity of Lévi-Strauss's socioeconomic theory—is an act not dissimilar to Jung's sense of surpassing the personal father to discover a spiritual father: a choice, in essence, of love over power as the mediating concern. It is all a matter of what we, as a society, choose to believe, and the images we choose to see as the reflections of our beliefs. The prevailing theory reflects the concerns and desires of the group that embraces it.

At present in the field of sociology, Claude Lévi-Strauss's theory has great influence. Lévi-Strauss is the most forthright of the theorists discussed in this chapter in his presentation of the incest prohibition as an issue of social and sexual power, though he shows no empathy for the inferior role of women in the social scheme he describes. He sees the incest prohibition simply as an issue of cultural, even economic, exchange: "The prohibition of incest is less a rule prohibiting marriage with the mother, sister, or daughter, than a rule obliging the mother, sister, or daughter to be given to others. It is the supreme rule of the gift" (1969, 481). Lévi-Strauss's language, his assumption that men are the active givers in society and women the appropriate objects of exchange, demonstrates his confidence in the persistence of the patriarchal social structure and his apparent comfort with the sexual division of roles within it. He explains away the possibility of early matriarchal cultures with a theory of an original disorganization of males:

> The "reign of women" is remembered only in mythology, an age, perhaps more simply, when men had not yet resolved the antinomy which is always likely to appear between their roles as takers of wives and givers of sisters, and making them both the authors and victims of their exchanges. (1969, 118)

Matriarchy, in Lévi-Strauss's conception, seems less a positive structure of female ascendency than a simple absence of male power before the men get their inevitable act together. We might ask in response to the above quote: *Who* are the victims of the exchanges the men make? The men themselves, or the women who have no say about their role as prime commodity in this social process? Lévi-Strauss seems to assume that men are the only victims and to disregard the emotional experience of women, perhaps because commodities do not have interior lives.

Lévi-Strauss speaks almost lyrically about the incest prohibition as a phenomenon by which "nature transcends itself" and which "brings about and is in itself the advent of a new order" (1969, 25). He places the incest prohibition at the intersection of nature and culture, participating in both and enabling humanity's transition from a brutal to a socialized condition.

> The alternative was between biological families living in juxtaposition and endeavoring to remain close, self-perpetuating units, over-ridden by their fears, hatred, and ignorances, and the systematic establishment, through the incest prohibition, of links of intermarriage between them, thus succeeding to build, out of the artificial bonds of affinity, a true human society, despite, and even in contradiction with, the isolating influence of consanguinity. (1956, 278)

Thus a continuous tradition exists from war to exchange, and from exchange to intermarriage, and the exchange of brides is merely the con-

82   IMAGINING INCEST

clusion to an uninterrupted process of reciprocal gifts, which effects the
transition from fear to friendship. (1969, 67–68)

Again, we might ask: Why are *women* the prime commodity in this
culture of exchange? Lévi-Strauss offers many reasons for women's
ultimate value, ranging from their traditional role as gatherers and
preparers of food (the more women, the more food on the table) to
the relative scarcity of sexually desirable women. Primitive cultures
maintain elaborate rules for the exchange of meats and other pre-
cious items, as well as observing the incest taboo requiring the exchange of women. But why then, within Lévi-Strauss's scheme, has
the incest prohibition remained so firmly in effect in our compara-
tively enlightened and affluent society? Because women persist as
the most valuable possession of men; women represent/embody/
signify for men the stimulation and satisfaction of sexual desire,
which has great value in itself but can also be deferred in favor of
cultural bonding with other men, as other human instincts, such as
eating, cannot be (Lévi-Strauss 1969, 62–63).

All this still does not explain why men exchange women, why men
are the actors and women the property, just as Herman points out
that so many studies of incest sidestep the question of why father-
daughter incest is, relative to mother-son incest, so much more frequent in occurrence. Boose offers one explanation in how Lévi-
Strauss's sense of the incest prohibition as "the supreme rule of the
gift" functions as a psychic euphemism in the male mind:

> Giving daughters . . . primary rights in themselves would threaten a psy-
> chic defense valuable to the father. The bestowal design places the
> daughter's departure from the father's house and her sexual union with
> another male into a text defined by obedience to her father—not prefer-
> ence for an outside male. So long as the strategy operates, the loss of a
> daughter can be psychologically integrated, and defeat by a rival male
> constructed into public rituals that redefine this transfer as the father's
> magnanimous gift. (Boose 1989, 32)

If this is the self-enhancing psychic experience for the father of the
incest prohibition and subsequent exchange of women, what is the
internal experience, the self-image developed by the women ex-
changed as commodities, as they gain awareness of their social role
as objects in such a self-serving patriarchal system? Presumably,
women poets would be most acutely afflicted by such a question, for
they would often be most conscious of their own subjective experi-

ence and aware of the nature of the social realm in which they try to express that experience. It seems inevitable that the rise of confessionalism as a poetic form in the middle of last century would be accompanied by an exploration in women's poetry of such a crisis in consciousness between the realm of personal experience and the social expectations encoded in the public medium of language. It also seems inevitable that incest would be the focus of such an exploration, for both the possibility of incest, particularly between father and daughter, and the prohibition against incest operate, at least on one level, to define women's subordinate place in a patriarchal society.

Lévi-Strauss himself speculates on the relation of the incest prohibition to language. He notes that the regulation against incest is most comprehensive in terms of social categories defined in language rather than in terms of biological relations:

> It is the social relationship more than the biological tie implied by the terms "father," "mother," "son," "daughter," "brother," and "sister," that acts as the determinant. . . . [T]he incest prohibition expresses the transition from the natural fact of consanguinity to the cultural fact of alliance. (1969, 30)

So Nabokov's Humbert Humbert, as stepfather of Lolita, pursues what is an incestuous relationship with her, despite the absence of a blood tie between them. It is incestuous, as Lolita herself knows, in part because society expects him to behave in the social role of father even if he is not Lolita's progenitor. The same situation applies to Orphan Annie and "Daddy" Warbucks. If, then, the incest prohibition forbids marriage or sexual contact between *socially* (and not just biologically) related individuals, identified in the titles conferred by language (as Sexton also implies in "The Death of the Fathers"), this rule might be creatively extended to question a woman's relationship to other father-figures in her patriarchal society, especially by a poet able to work with the incest motif symbolically.

Lévi-Strauss seems to acknowledge this possibility at the end of *Elementary Structures of Kinship*: "The incest prohibition is universal like language. . . . [T]he relations between the sexes can be conceived as one of the modalities of a great 'communication function' which also includes language" (1969, 493–94). But Lévi-Strauss's concept of language fails to recognize the potential for creative play with social structures in poetry. As a social scientist, he seems to be aware only of the denotations of words and to reduce their affective value even below that of the prime commodity, women:

> In contrast to words, which have wholly become signs, woman has re-mained at once a sign and a value. This explains why the relations be-tween the sexes have preserved that affective richness, ardour and mystery which doubtless originally permeated the entire universe of human communications. (1969, 496)

The final sentences of *Elementary Structures of Kinship* present a vision of paradise that indulges the human impulse to hoard:

> To this very day, mankind has always dreamed of seizing and fixing that fleeting moment when it was permissible to believe that the law of ex-change could be evaded, that one could gain without losing, enjoy with-out sharing. . . . a world in which one might *keep to oneself.* (1969, 496–97)

If Lévi-Strauss could open up the connotations of "mankind" to in-clude an empathetic view of woman's role in this system of ex-change, he might be able to appreciate some of the efforts by women of this era to redefine social relationships through creative presentations of the incest motif in poetry, and to reconcile their social status as commodities with their subjective experiences as de-siring individuals. Lévi-Strauss is aware that our society has largely abandoned the gift as the means of exchange (1969, 61), and he notes a recent tendency toward hoarding rather than sharing (1969, 47)—both trends reflected in Eunice, who, in essence, marries hap-pily into her father's bank, and in Sexton's Orphan Annie and "Daddy" Warbucks. Our society of affluence might seem to have transcended the need for more generalized forms of the prohibition against incest and at times almost to favor, subliminally at least, the family's tendency to keep the women and the money to itself—not to have to share. This is the more fluid social reality that Sexton, Plath, and other women poets have been probing through the incest motif in their poetry. What might come of the incest prohibition in terms of an improvement in the social role of women? Anything might be preferable to the status of most valued commodity. The daughter-poet might even learn to use the father-imago to enable her own desires, as Sharon Olds does.

As this chapter has shown, both psychology and sociology have ex-plored the issue of power in the experience of incest itself and in the social prohibition against incest. In both disciplines, incest or its prohibition has been seen both as a mechanism of woman's subjection and as a potential tool for her liberation. But male scholars who know by direct experience only one side of the issue must be complemented by female poets who feel the other. Woman's subjective experience of the pervasive reality of incest—physical and, even more, psychological—can be illuminated only by women who can explore that realm creatively, not comment on it analytically from a distance. Mary Daly has argued that it is precisely because women know intimately the position of primary designated other, scapegoat, or commodity in a patriarchal society (as even Lacan acknowledges), that it must be women who will lead society away from the limitations of patriarchy and toward a more fully equalized structure in which certain groups do not suffer to maintain a self-image of well-being in the prevailing group.

> It is women who are conditioned to be the internalizers *par excellence.* . . . Realizing this fact, women have a clue to an essential dynamic involved in uprooting the prevailing sense of reality. This is to expel what has been internalized, to recognize that such structures are in some sense less real than our own dreams. (Daly 1973, 136)

In the following chapters we will see how Adrienne Rich and Sharon Olds have redefined their relations with the fathers of society. Their efforts differ, and Rich's rebellion seems to be needed before Olds's redefinition of the Father is possible, but both poets look at the social and emotional experiences of women from the inside out, seeking to center themselves in a world in which they live as fully functioning subjects.

3

Adrienne Rich and the
Politics of Separation

We have had enough suicidal women poets, enough suicidal women, enough of self-destructiveness as the sole form of violence permitted to women. . . . When we begin to feel compassion for ourselves and each other instead of for our rapists, we will begin to be immune to suicide. (Rich 1979, 122)

THESE WORDS BY ADRIENNE RICH, SPOKEN IN A MEMORIAL FOR ANNE Sexton and also in memory of Sylvia Plath, may serve as an introduction to Rich's radical response to the patriarchal expectations for women outlined in the previous chapter. Rich was once as eager to win a place in the male poetic tradition as were Sexton and especially Plath, by compliance with traditional poetic structures and themes. (Plath and Rich were, notably, both enamored of Yeats's poetry early in their poetic careers.) But by mid-career, Rich rejected the male tradition as too compromising to her integrity as a woman poet; she realized the costs of compliance much more quickly than did Sexton and Plath, in part because she survived them and learned from their example.

Rich learned from Sexton and Plath what *not* to do in poetry, how *not* to court the favor of the male powers to win acceptance and success. Sexton and Plath began to rebel against conventional expectations with complaints of abuse from fathers and father-surrogates, and Plath opened up the category of abusers to include all men, but neither woman found a way to separate from the men they identified as abusive. After an initial period of compliance, Adrienne Rich

---

Note—I do not quote from the poetry of Adrienne Rich in this chapter, or elsewhere in this book, since she has denied me permission to do so. Instead I paraphrase the poems I discuss. I encourage the reader to read those poems in their original sources, to which I will refer for convenience throughout the chapter.

began her condemnation of men as a group, where Plath left off. When Rich turns to this topic in her poetry, she condemns patriarchy in general and all men who benefit from and participate in that social structure. Only much later in her life does she confront her own father in her poems as the origin of her repudiation of patriarchy. The "we" of Rich's critical prose and of most of her poetry is female; she has developed her own sense of a woman-centered culture, and she advocates lesbianism as a crucial alternative to what she calls "compulsory heterosexuality"—"heterosexuality as a political institution which disempowers women" (1986a, 34–35). For Rich, lesbianism is "both the breaking of a taboo and the rejection of a compulsory way of life. . . . [It is] a form of naysaying to patriarchy, an act of resistance" (52). Since men, according to Rich, "insofar as they are embodiments of the patriarchal idea[,] have become dangerous to children and other living things, themselves included" (1979, 83–84), the lesbian assumes a crucial role in society, as the antithesis, even the antidote to the patriarchal male: "It is the lesbian in us who is creative, for the dutiful daughter of the fathers in us is only a hack" (201).

In many respects, Adrienne Rich revives the specter of Sappho in modern culture. Rich, like Sexton and Plath and many other poets, has used the enigmatic figure of Sappho to reflect her own most prominent concerns. A young and very ambitious Sylvia Plath ranked Sappho as the first among her rivals for poetic fame (Plath 1982, 211), and Anne Sexton toward the end of her life wrote a poem about a modern Sappho that reveals Sexton's own interest in literary fame as well as her dread of losing conventional supports in pursuit of it ("The Red Dance," 1981, 530–31). To Rich, Sappho is a poetic foremother (1979, 39), someone who may help her decipher the optimal female response to a male-dominated world. In this regard, the highly fragmentary nature of Sappho's poetic canon is a reminder of the "destruction of records and memorabilia and letters documenting the realities of lesbian experience . . . as a means of keeping heterosexuality compulsory for women" (1986a, 52). Sappho's surviving writings, which seem to document her involvement in a lesbian community, give Rich hope for a reconnection of creative, loving sisters, both those alive today and those who have lived over the millennia (53, 55). Rich believes that our cultural memory of Sappho must spur us to recreate today some of the ideals of the early matriarchal cultures, which so many male scholars, like Levi-Strauss, have doubted or derided (1986a, 227).

Sappho scholar Joan DeJean has demonstrated that the subjective images that Plath, Sexton, and Rich have projected onto Sappho constitute a familiar response (1989, 3). Since the time of Ovid, who first created an image of her to suit his own poetic ambitions, Sappho has been continuously recreated as a symbol of desire—the desire embodied in her poetry becoming the projecting poet's own desire. The paucity of historical information on Sappho and the fragmented and very limited nature of her surviving poetry both enable this transmutation of Sappho from historical being into literary symbol. Interestingly, it is only in recent decades that Sappho has come to bear the image of lesbian poet exclusively. DeJean makes it clear that Sappho's extant poetry and what we know of her life do not finally determine the sexual orientation of her poetic persona, much less her historical person (1989, 20–21); her poems can be read as celebrating either heterosexual or homosexual love or both.

Earlier, premodern images of Sappho have clustered in three groups: first is a chaste woman poet with a lesbian courtesan double; second is a poet who was also a conventional heterosexual woman; third (beginning with Ovid and most popular of all) is a lesbian poet who falls in love with a younger man in her later years, is spurned by him, and in turn renounces all her prior female loves and throws herself off a cliff to her death in the sea—a woman who learns to conform to sexual norms too late and is punished for her arrogance (DeJean 1989, 46). These images, however, are all creations of men who have, as DeJean puts it, "ventriloquized" Sappho. The few women who have taken over Sappho's image for their own poetic purposes have imagined her as a strongly independent woman in order to "become able to assume the literarily deviant role of woman writer" (DeJean 1989, 6). But the male images have prevailed over time, creating the legend of a woman that affirms, sooner or later, the heterosexual norm of society—what Rich herself calls the institution of heterosexuality. As DeJean clarifies, all these male fictions of Sappho have in common the effects of separating "female sexuality and poetic genius" and "humilat[ing] the woman in order to assume control over her literary legacy" (17). Over two and one half millennia after Sappho's death, female poets, like the four studied in this text, are still battling such reductive male images of Sappho, the archetypal female poet. In essence, the historical commodification of Sappho by men mirrors much of the damage done to women's self-image by such reductive male depictions of women as we see in the writings of Freud and Lévi-Strauss. It is this damage that Rich seeks to correct and prevent.

The modern image of Sappho is, however, strongly lesbian (De-Jean 1989, 306), and it is this image that Rich is able to draw on, mostly indirectly, for the strength of traditional precedent. Notably, Sappho's modern image seems to come closer than earlier male images to the poet's original cultural status, in that it does not subordinate her to some male ideal. Sappho was to her contemporaries " '*the* poetess,' the female counterpart, and presumably the equal of '*the* poet,' Homer" (DeJean 1989, 1). Another classics scholar, Page DuBois, carries this assessment even further, celebrating Sappho from the perspective of modern hindsight as among the first writers of all Western culture to step away from the more primitive, male-bonded tribalism portrayed by Homer into a new perspective of personal subjectivity, speaking and feeling as "I":

> We see in the work of Sappho the very beginnings of . . . the construction of selfhood, of the fiction of subjectivity, at its origins. The community of Homeric heroes, of men feasting around a camp fire, dividing up the spoils of battle—spoils which included the women of the conquered people—conceived of identity as a collective. . . . Sappho is a crucial figure in this process of separating out individuality from the communal mass of pre-urban society. Her poetic representations of desire and subjectivity, of an "I" that sings and wills, that suffers jealousy and longing, begin to open up a space for private, interior life, a life that will not be realized for centuries to come. (1991, 13–14)

Thus DuBois presents Sappho as a woman celebrating her own subjectivity, her own desires and frustrations, as opposed to the Homeric presentation of women as the spoils of battle, which Lévi-Strauss later builds on as his image of social reality. DeJean also argues that Sappho is a kind of proto-postmodernist figure, in that she anticipates the renunciation in much postmodern art and culture of patriarchal limitations that cluster around the basic duality of the privileged, dominant male and his subordinates.

Rich shares this modern feminist appreciation of Sappho, but Sappho's more traditional representations betray the difficulties a lesbian feminist poet like Rich must face in her art and life. DeJean shows convincingly that Sappho has been used by aspiring male authors as a commodity to facilitate male poetic bonding in literary activities, in a manner very similar to the male exchange of women described by Lévi-Strauss.

Sappho has known a fate unique in literary tradition: for centuries, her reputation has been grounded in her exceptional value as literary property, that is, her ability to function repeatedly in an age-old tradition of male poetic exchanges. . . . [M]ale poets strive to take over the powerful desire for woman she had originated, to put their poet figures in the place of Sappho's speaking subject. . . . Sappho is passed from man to man as an accessory in a detour of desire by which a series of male poets position themselves with respect to each other. . . . This need to keep poetic authority under male control . . . also says that a female "I" will not have the power to dictate the form of erotic poetry. (1989, 29, 36, 38)

DeJean suggests that the usurpation and commodification of Sappho's image by male poets was provoked by the very strength and self-sufficiency of the female community many of Sappho's poems depict. Ironically, DeJean speaks of exchange again, but this time of an exchange *among* rather than *of* women. This is an image of a matriarchal community denied by Lévi-Strauss in his description of the exchange of women as prime commodity.

Sappho portrays both the composition and performance of her verse as an exchange among women, as the product of a female community whose members are united by bonds both personal and professional. . . . Yet this female bond can be considered in purely literary terms as an attempt to bypass male literary authority and to deny men any primary role in the process of poetic creation. Sappho presents poetic creation as a gift handed down from woman to woman, as literature written by women for other women and about other women. In this poetic universe, males are relegated to a peripheral, if not an intrusive, role. Most strikingly, the Sapphic narrator, a woman, repeatedly assumes a classically male prerogative. She is the desiring subject. (DeJean 1989, 47–48)

No wonder Sappho is of great interest to Rich—this image of Sappho and her community of women strongly counters the psychoanalytic and sociological images of women as objects of male desire discussed in the previous chapter. In fact, it seems to show an early but strong alternative or complement to patriarchy, which Rich would like to see reconstituted today. Moreover, from DuBois's perspective, Sappho is the original desiring subject—she is a creator of the role, not a usurper of it. The position would become "classically male" only after its appropriation by those male poets who have repackaged Sappho for their own consumption. What DuBois and DeJean show is that male poets from Ovid to the present have recognized the prime value in poetry of the desiring subject and have acted to deny that role to Sappho (and thus all woman poets) and claim it for themselves. It was only with the rise of confessional poetry last century that Sexton, Plath, and Rich could strongly resume the role of desiring subject. Adrienne Rich, especially in the middle period of her poetry, celebrates like Sappho a community of women as the preferred, creative cultural form and tries to push men out to the periphery, as Sexton and Plath are never able to do.

In a Sapphic poem a recent translator entitles "So I Called to Aphrodite," the speaker identifies herself as Sappho and calls on Aphrodite, goddess of love, to assist in her most recent love affair. The one adjective in the poem that would identify the loved persona as male or female is not clear in any extant version of the poem (DeJean 1989, 319–20); thus, translators have read the loved one as male or female depending on their own preferences. Modern translators have opted for the female designation, at least in part because so many of the other poems do identify the loved one as female. But there is also evidence within the poem itself for this identification. The manner in which Sappho addresses Aphrodite suggests a preference for female companionship in contrast to male modes of social interaction. In the beginning and ending of the poem, parts directly addressed to Aphrodite, Sappho asks the goddess to leave her father's house and to be her "Helper in Battle" (Sappho 1991, 59). Military battles are more the affair of Zeus and Homer, whereas Sappho's battle is personal, internal, one of emotions. Sappho calls on Aphrodite to leave the patriarchal realm of battle as Homer has depicted it, in order to assist Sappho in her very different love conflicts. Sappho seems to argue indirectly that the male world of power and war must be left behind for the female realm of love. In this reading, it would be more natural for the loved one to be female also, and not a male from the world of the fathers.

In the beginning of another poem, Sappho quite openly distinguishes her pleasures from the male world of military displays, rejecting various configurations of soldiers in preference for the loved one (83). Similarly, in her marriage poems, Sappho often openly depicts traditional marriage as conquest and economic exchange, in line with Lévi-Strauss's sense of society. Sappho's preference for a loving and cultured community of women over the conquest mentality of men seems to point to a greater pleasure in loving what one has than in trading it to strengthen one's bond with another in a social power structure. In a symbolic sense, the subjectivity pre-

sented in Sappho's poetry is more incestuous than the male orientation toward exchange, which suggests (as we saw in regard to
Durkheim's theory in chapter 2) that not all effects of the incest
taboo are beneficial to women. Sappho writes of her daughter in
terms that openly contradict the father's traditional use of the
daughter as a "gift" to another man, but demonstrating instead
great love and respect. She protests that even various realms would
not be a tempting "exchange" for her daughter (87).

⁀

In much of her prose and poetry, Adrienne Rich tries, Sappho-
like, to turn away from the patriarchal presences in her life and to
create a loving community of women. But for a woman whose poetic
talent was actively nurtured by her father and who married a man
and bore three sons, this was at first not an easy or obvious goal.
Indeed, it was apparently the experience of bearing three sons in
five years immediately following college that radicalized Rich away
from compliance and toward rebellion; she would later say, "under
patriarchy, female possibility has been literally massacred on the site
of motherhood" (1976, 13). Rich has provided her readers with
more information about her personal life, in both prose and poetry,
than nearly any other contemporary poet. (In this respect, her persona is quite the opposite to what we have left of Sappho.) She has
done this in part because she sees her life as representative, both of
the problems of being a woman today and of the possibilities for
solutions to many of these problems. Rich has noted that her coming to self-awareness coincided with the first peak of the woman's
liberation movement in the early 1970s; it was in this period also
that her father died and that Rich left her husband and assumed her
lesbian identity. Her life has, in a sense, shown in microcosm the
modern evolution of female consciousness, in its journey from compliance to liberation. Rich would later say that she discovered a mission in her life to alter the rules of history (1986b, 23). Because
there is so much material available by Rich on the theme of daughter and father and, more broadly, women and men, and because
Rich sees her life as representative, it is helpful to look at her prose
and poetry within developmental stages: the childhood submission
of daughter to father and the compliance of the adult daughter with
patriarchal expectations; the rebellion of the self-defined woman
against patriarchal limitations; and the somewhat tentative reaching

of the mature woman toward a kind of collegiality or mutual recognition between women and men, at least those who have worked free of patriarchal definitions.

Rich's portrait of her childhood is consistent throughout her prose and poetry. It is a portrait of privilege, especially in terms of parental attention—a privilege apparently appreciated by the young child, but later viewed much more cynically by the self-conscious woman.

> *A poet's education.* A white child growing into her powers of language within white discourse. Every day when she is about five years old, her father sets her a few lines of poetry to copy into a ruled notebook as a handwriting lesson. She receives a written word in her notebook as grade: "Excellent," "Very good," "Good," "Fair," "Poor." (1993c, 182)

As this passage shows, Rich's early relationship with her father was intense but mixed. He was her muse, in a sense; he had faith in her abilities, inspired her to greater and greater accomplishment, and gave her a great deal of attention and response. But he was also her critic, judging her work by how well it mimicked what he considered to be the best, whether in handwriting, metrics, or subject matter. He praised the child's skillful assimilation. Eventually, Rich came to see the harmful as well as the beneficial effects of her father's rigorous attention to her work.

> He prowled and pounced over my school papers, . . . he criticized my poems for faulty technique and gave me books on rhyme and meter and form. His investment in my intellect and talent was egotistical, tyrannical, opinionated, and terribly wearing. He taught me, nevertheless, to believe in hard work, to mistrust easy inspiration, to write and rewrite; to feel that I *was* a person of the book, even though a woman; to take ideas seriously. (1986a, 113)

Rich realized as an adult, "I never in my whole life knew what my father was really feeling" (1986a, 113). It took a while for Rich to learn how to know what she was really feeling as well. The good daughter who developed to please that ambitious father was at first as adept at reproducing the achievements of high culture and as unaware of her own feelings as he was—she was what Rich herself has called a "token" woman.

The poetry of Rich's first two volumes, *A Change of World* (1951) and *The Diamond Cutters* (1955), embodies the ambivalence of this good daughter. Titles and topics question, even reach for rebellion; the first poem of the first volume is entitled, prophetically, "Storm Warnings." Clearly, Rich's persona announces that all is not well, that something must "change," but she does not have the self-awareness or the tools to identify what is wrong or what changes must be made. Despite this veneer of protest, the poems are deeply ambiguous, entrenched in the expectations of culture to the extent that Rich speaks in anything but her own voice. Her speakers are male, often old and even dying men—the voice of patriarchy itself; or some omniscient "we," unidentified by any characteristic of sex or age or race; or, if female, a woman in a love relationship with a man, not speaking for herself alone. There are many literary allusions to established great male poets, especially to W. B. Yeats—a kind of bowing to the poetic patriarchy, as we also see in Plath's early poetry. In the end, the voice of the first two volumes is more compliant than rebellious. When later preparing her *Collected Early Poems*, Rich wrote that various poems in *The Diamond Cutters* use poetic technique and allusion to subvert the poet's personal voice (1993a, xix). Her first efforts to find meaning, order, and power in poetry were methods learned from her father and male poetic predecessors, not an indigenous, "native" (as she will later term it in a volume title) effort at understanding.

Even the much-anthologized "Aunt Jennifer's Tigers" (1993a, 4) depicts Aunt Jennifer's unhappiness with her role in a patriarchal society only through her art. The tigers she creates with her needlework never jump out of the frame, and she dies with her heavy wedding band still in place. Any rebellion that occurs in these early poems occurs only allegorically, in the realm of imagination and art; the social status quo is left unchanged. In a poem that could well be read today as depicting the uncertainties of recovered memory syndrome, "What Ghosts Can Say" (1993a, 7), an anonymous speaker observes a young boy's fear of his father's ghost, but only questions what such a situation means; the poem itself draws no conclusions. Other poems, such as "The Uncle Speaks in the Drawing Room" (1993a, 24), present the uncle as the embodiment of patriarchy, uncannily like Freud's frequent substitution of uncle for father in his early case histories of incest. Rich seems almost as unwilling to endanger her potentially rewarding relation to social structures by questioning the father's abuse of power as Freud was. Uncles, ghosts of fathers, and later in *The Diamond Cutters* a collective group of fathers (1993a, 65)—all speak for a society that condemns and re-

presses the independent thoughts or acts of its daughters, but Rich
does not yet assume the confessional mode and examine directly
her own hopes and desires or her relation to her own father.

A brief, precisely balanced poem, "An Unsaid Word" (1993a, 28),
portrays the necessary social role of any woman hoping to be accepted. It depicts the woman who learns not to impose on her man's
wandering thoughts, even though she has the power to do so.
Rather, she remains where his thoughts have left her, awaiting the
return of his attention. This poem is so accomplished in technique
and male-oriented in perspective, it could be the work of Yeats. And
that is probably what Rich hoped to accomplish in these early
poems—to join the ranks of the great poets of the past by mirroring
their efforts. Yet she knows, obscurely, that even though she can
speak the language of belonging, she is "By No Means Native," the
title of a poem on one of her male poetic subjects (1993a, 13). When
she points to problems of ghosts and assimilation, she speaks
through or of male experience, not admitting the problems as her
own. When, in "For the Conjunction of Two Planets" (1993a, 54),
Rich presents a potentially positive feminist image of Venus and Ju-
piter as the dominant female planet and a subordinate male planet,
she will not step into the social or political implications of that
image, preferring to leave the message in the sky. Realization and
rebellion are safely left in the realm of imagination, like Aunt Jennifer's tigers.

Rich's first two volumes thus embody her dilemma—the dilemma
of feeling subconsciously as a woman the wrongs of patriarchy but
confronting them only in the realm of imagination and otherwise
openly bowing to the fathers of culture and poetry, who potentially
have so much to grant an aspiring poet and good daughter. The
problem is that restricting awareness to the realm of imagination
allows for ongoing and disabling social complicity, as we have seen
in the poems of Sexton and Plath. In Rich's "Living in Sin" (1993a,
94), a young woman partly realizes that she is being used as a convenience by the man she lives with—this, and not their unmarried
state, is the "sin" she lives in. But she maintains this degrading situation because of the romantic promises she carries in her mind; she
cannot reject this reality as long as she retreats into fantasy and lives
in hope that the relationship will someday conform to that fantasy.
This paradox applies as well to the author of this poem, who also
cannot deal with reality if she fantasizes being incorporated into the
poetic canon with Yeats and the other great poetic forefathers.

Rich is quite open in her prose about her compliant position in this first stage of her adult life. She acknowledges that as she became independent from her family, entering college and then marriage, she wanted to retain her father's intense commitment to her, but on her terms.

> I wanted him to cherish and approve of me, not as he had when I was a child, but as the woman I was, who had her own mind and had made her own choices. This, I finally realized, was not to be; Arnold [her father] demanded absolute loyalty, absolute submission to his will. . . . I was learning in concrete ways a great deal about patriarchy, in particular how the "special" woman, the favored daughter, is controlled and rewarded. (1986a, 116)

Rich's marriage to another Jew strayed too far from her father's desire for assimilation and caused a break in their relations, almost literally the paternal "abandonment" that Marion Woodman identifies as necessary to provoke the quest toward independence in the creative daughter. Indeed, Rich has described this period of her life in terms of a break from a psychologically incestuous relationship with her father: "This 'perfect' daughter, though gratifyingly precocious, . . . had finally resisted her father's Victorian paternalism, his seductive charm and controlling cruelty. . . . She had ceased to be the demure and precocious child or the poetic, seducible adolescent" (1976, 223).

However, Rich's marriage to a man not unlike her father suggests that even though she consciously rebelled against her own father and his social expectations for her, she was still, early in her marriage and early in her career as a poet, quite compliant within the larger patriarchal system, which she hoped would accept her as an "honorary boy" (Herman and Hirschman 1982, 57). Rich says of herself at the time of her first pregnancy:

> I still identified more with men than with women; the men I knew seemed less held back by self-doubt and ambivalence, more choices seemed open to them. I wanted to give birth, at twenty-five, to my unborn self, the self that our father-centered family had suppressed in me, someone independent, actively willing, original. . . . If I wanted to give birth to myself as a male, it was because males seemed to inherit those qualities by right of gender. (1976, 193)

Rich's early career thus runs parallel to the evolving work of Sexton and Plath. All three were struggling at about the same time (in the

1950s and 1960s) with their own poetic ambitions and the counter-manding messages of the poetic establishment on what was accept-able in poetry, especially from a woman. All three tried the route of self-abnegating compliance, like Electra; Adrienne Rich's distinc-tion is that she broke most cleanly away from that route. Whereas Plath spent her last months in a house previously tenanted by Yeats and died there, Rich tempered her admiration for Yeats and the po-etic patriarchy, realizing that such compliance robbed her of too much of herself.

The bulk of Rich's poetry—from her third volume, *Snapshots of a Daughter-in-Law* (1963), through her ninth volume, *A Wild Patience Has Taken Me This Far* (1981)—records her evolution away from an early Electra orientation and toward a more mature Sapphic stance. What marks these volumes is not only an open and angry rejection of all males participating in patriarchy and of her own degraded role options in that system, but also an embracing love for women, both lesbian sexual love and the spiritual love of a community of women. As with DuBois's vision of Sappho, Rich depicts women as walking the more enlightened path, leaving men back in the darker realms of preconscious instinct. Charlotte Wolff, a psychiatrist who has stud-ied lesbians, has found that "the lesbian has never accepted the status of an object" (1971, 66). This strong self-image is, however, built out of conflict with her parents:

> Even as an only child, the girl cannot get over the suspicion that her mother would be more profoundly loving towards her if she were a boy. Competition with the male is one of the principal causes of her rejection of him. By resenting the male as a rival, either in reality or in imagina-tion, she identifies with him and tries to outdo him. . . . She wants to be the one who chooses, and cannot accept that he wants to make her feel a chosen object. The core of an independent personality finds a good opportunity for growth in this atmosphere of self-assertion and aggres-sion. (1971, 68)

Significantly, in this second stage of her poetic evolution, Rich be-gins to deal with her personal father in her poetry and prose, but his complex presence in her creative life, as antagonist and muse, is not deeply explored. The deeper conflicts are mostly hidden in her more generalized messages to patriarchy.

In the foreword to her *Collected Early Poems*, Adrienne Rich identifies *Snapshots of a Daughter-in-Law* as the volume in which she began to deal with her own experience and not the imagined experience of insiders (1993a, xix). What prompted Rich's turn to self-analysis in poetry, after great public success with her more formal and traditional early poems, was her own experience of motherhood, or more precisely her own great disillusionment in the experience of motherhood: "Motherhood is 'sacred' so long as its offspring are 'legitimate'—that is, as long as the child bears the name of a father who legally controls them" (1976, 42). Rich's poems, however, show that such philosophical certainty was hard-won. The multi-part poem "Snapshots of a Daughter-in-Law" (1993a, 145–49) struggles with conflicting images of self and other women in history and literature.

Does an adult woman possess herself, or is she better defined as "daughter-in-law"? The woman who thought she had achieved independence from her father by marrying finds that she has changed only from biological daughter to daughter "in law" of many father-surrogates, from husband to husband's father to rabbi to poet. Rich was able to find a route out of that subordination only by stepping out of the system itself, the same system she had so recently sought to star in.

> Much of the first four decades of my life was spent in a continuous tension between the world the Fathers taught me to see, and had rewarded me for seeing, and the flashes of insight that came through the eye of the outsider. . . . It was only when I could finally affirm the outsider's eye as the source of a legitimate and coherent vision, that I began to be able to do the work I truly wanted to do, live the kind of life I truly wanted to live, instead of carrying out the assignments I had been given as a privileged woman and a token. (1986a, 3–4)

Rich describes in this quote her evolution in consciousness from object to subject and her awareness that her own subjectivity placed her as an outsider in patriarchal society. Her courage of vision allowed her to turn the tables on the male insiders and label them as outside her system of values, much as we see in Sappho's poems. In this way, Rich in effect refused rescue by an ideal male and acted to rescue herself, avoiding Electra's fate.

In *Snapshots of a Daughter-in-Law*, the father is still present as an enforcing agent, both in the abstract and in memory of personal experience—the internal imago that governs Rich's adult thoughts and acts, just as the actual father governed her in childhood. She remembers sitting at her father's desk and writing poems for her father and other relatives and friends to read. It is not presented as a willing activity of the child, though she is obedient (1993a, 156). The grown daughter in turn struggles to find the meaning of her misery in the midst of such apparent privilege (1993a, 183). Slowly, through an agonized self-scrutiny, Rich's persona (always now female and subjective) begins to pull away from the system that degrades her. This progress seems necessarily to involve a growing gap between herself and her husband, the primary father-substitute, which is nicely captured in imagery of different time zones in "The Lag" (1993a, 190). She has flown off into a new reality and can no longer communicate easily with her husband, who has been left behind.

As Rich's persona pulls off into a world of her own reality and sees her husband from a distance, still back where she began, she is also able to stand back somewhat from old memories and images of her father and to acknowledge to some extent both their differences and their relatedness. In "After Dark" (1993a, 227–29), a remarkable poem written four years before her father's death, Rich celebrates her developing sense of identity in terms of release from and equality with her father. The title seems to refer more to her own liberation than to her father's approaching death, though she is clearly concerned about that; there is more sense of achievement than loss in the poem. "After Dark" seems to achieve an early insight into the potentially rewarding relatedness of fathers and daughters, to which Rich will not return for many more years. It should be read carefully and in full. Toward the beginning of the poem, Rich recalls her father's authoritarian role in her childhood, his efforts to supercede her own knowledge of herself with his own knowledge of her, to reduce her to the role of subordinate. She then reviews her efforts to leave him and find herself, only to discover that she is still his daughter, still of his blood. Now that she's strong enough to grapple with him as an equal, he is weakening with age, and this frustrates Rich. She wants their struggles to continue. The poem includes endearing words and images for the father. Their relationship is clearly still important to Rich, not one to be discarded or left behind.

If this is the self-possessed daughter, fully alive, confronting her father, it is also the daughter seeking to lead the father to a new life of strength in their relationship. Daughter does not want father to fade to nothing now that she is more his equal counterpart; she wants to try her strength in sparring with him. So she leads him through a death of old images to resurrection in a new form she can openly struggle with. This poem not only evokes Plath's and Sexton's poems about their fathers, it also anticipates Sharon Olds's creative struggles with the father-imago in her poetry. In the next five volumes of poetry, Rich's personal father virtually disappears again, as the poet openly and strongly struggles with patriarchy in many other forms and embraces an independent sexual, political, and cultural identity as a lesbian. It is as if Rich in "After Dark" recasts the imago of her father, turning him from the broken record that insists on her subservience to a separate person, related but no longer in control of her. The new imago, which Rich calls a "dream," is tolerant if not openly supportive; it thus frees the daughter in her journey.

Subsequent poems will show that Rich has not settled with patriarchy in "After Dark," but has rather found a new set of images with which to negotiate parental relationships. Once free of the dominance of father, she can focus more clearly on her relationship with mother, every child's first love. As we have seen in chapter 2, Gayle Rubin argues that all children do initially seek love in the mother and thus most naturally in women, but that young girls are resocialized to prefer their fathers and then men in general, to prepare them for their subordinate role in the patriarchal social order. This is Rich's position as well. She comes to see the romance of heterosexual love as a cruel social trick played on females in order to compel their participation in patriarchy. But she also acts to free herself from the effects of this deception. As Rich's Terrible Father dies in "After Dark" and is replaced by a much less intrusive imago, Rich recovers her original love for the mother.

Rich's improved relations with her father-imago do not, however, extend to other men. During the 1970s, in the second stage of Rich's poetic evolution, she denounces men inclusively while establishing herself as a feminist and a lesbian. In 1971 she refers to the "self-destructiveness of male-dominated society" and in 1979 to the "lies and distortions of the culture men have devised" (1979, 35, 12). She sees lesbians as functioning historically as the last holdouts against the evils of patriarchy. Rich makes clear that her choice of lesbianism was not a matter of biological determinism (1986a, viii n. 1) but, although not consciously political, perhaps a "nascent" political act

(66). For Rich, living as a lesbian is a learned choice, or perhaps a relearned choice, in that it involves a return to the original woman-love for the mother that patriarchy attempts to strip from all women. To become a lesbian is to bypass the patriarchal imperative of heterosexuality and the related incest taboo, much as we have seen in Sappho's love for her daughter and other women. Wolff has in fact defined lesbianism as "emotional incest with the mother" and as the woman's "desire to re-establish a lost paradise—the union with her mother" (1971, 60), and emphasizes that lesbian relationships are marked by idealism and emotionality even more than by sexual choice. Rich adds that such an idealistic desire for reunion does not have to stop with a sexual relationship between two people—that a more communal kind of lesbian awareness has constructive rewards for all women:

> I mean the term *lesbian continuum* to include a range—through each woman's life and throughout history—of woman-identified experience, not simply the fact that a woman has had or consciously desired genital sexual experience with another woman. If we expand it to embrace many more forms of primary intensity between and among women, including the sharing of a rich inner life, the bonding against male tyranny, . . . we begin to grasp breadths of female history and psychology which have lain out of reach as a consequence of limited, mostly clinical, definitions of *lesbianism.* (1986a, 51–52)

The poems of this middle period turn away from technical displays of talent and also often from subtleties of subject. The poem "Rape," from *Diving into the Wreck,* opens bluntly, with reference to a predatory cop who is also a father (1973, 44). Many of the poems seem intent on achieving a non-poetic, non-metaphorical, rather black-and-white image of reality. As Rich puts it in the title poem, this is an attempt to see the reality and not the stories that have been written, usually by men, about that reality (23). Conventional poetic language is mistrusted as part of the patriarchal system, as enforcing that system; poetry must become almost non-poetic to speak the outsider's truth. At the same time, Rich has not yet fully divorced herself from the female/male duality of patriarchal thought. When she looks for strength to name her own experience, she occasionally still seeks male figures, as in the poem "Orion" (1993a, 283–84). Rich calls to the constellation as her king and brother, and she casts her own desires up into the sky to escape her own misery on earth. The

final line of "Orion" suggests that Rich is aware of the irony of trying to escape her entrapment in the patriarchal system by calling on
an image stuck in the sky, a male image at that. But clearly she is
searching for a source of power to draw on, and for that she must
look outside her "normal" life as wife and mother. In "The Stelae"
(1993a, 388), Rich looks for answers from some strange inscribed
stones—perhaps like the tablets that bear the Ten Commandments,
laws of the Father—that her dead father possesses in a dream she
has of him. But these potentially oracular objects, like the phallic
power of the Father, are still in his possession, and she waits passively
and even wistfully for him to pass them on. And all the while, the
"Demon Lover" (1993a, 291–94), like a vulture in the seductive, romantic myth of patriarchy, waits to reclaim Rich's struggling persona.

The poems in *The Dream of a Common Language* (1978) and *A Wild
Patience Has Taken Me This Far* (1981) are the most women-centered
and lesbian-oriented of all Rich's poetry. The power and love of
women are often presented as contrary to male prerogatives, much
as Sappho so often presents them. To depict such womanly love and
power, Rich essentially rewrites the patriarchal myth. In "Splittings"
(1978, 10–11), Rich refuses to retreat into the protective mother by
way of her lover (the emotional incest with mother described by
Wolff), for she sees that as a prerogative claimed by males or a refuge sought by powerless women. She looks, rather, for power and
love in combination.

Woman-love, mother-love, sister-love—all are redefined in these
volumes as acts of strength, not the failures or perversions the patriarchal system brands them. In "Sibling Mysteries" (1978, 47–52), a
poem for her sister, Rich reviews the negative consequences of the
patriarchal system on the women in a family, and offers new interpretations of their relations. The final lines rewrite Freudian psychology in their assertion of the primary bond of the daughter with
the mother, not the father, and the primacy of the continuing bonds
of women with each other. Even the possibility of the empathic man
is derided, for that is the greatest temptation of the romantic myth
that helps to sustain patriarchy (1978, 62). Rich here no longer projects her wish for power onto Orion or her dead father. She has
found a female source of power.

The achievement of the poems of this middle period is that they
offer alternative readings of reality; the limitation of these poems is
that male-female relations often become stereotyped. In the final

poem in *The Dream of a Common Language,* "Transcendental Etude" (1978, 72–77), it becomes almost deadeningly inevitable that the viciously wounded animal is female and that the male hunter is drunk and inept, not a careful marksman culling a herd. Evil is too easily projected out of the female self and onto the male other, resulting in rather flat and frozen images of both and reproducing too easily in reverse the common patriarchal stereotypes of females. Why should not it be, rather, that the male role has served its purpose (hunting was once necessary for the survival of all) and that female strengths are now reviving to meet new needs and opportunities? Does one strength have to obliterate the other? Rich will deal with these questions in the next stage of her poetic career, but this stage ends with her hope for evolution resting in women alone. She speaks of learning to love herself through the love of another woman and of the new world of poetry that opens with this experience (1978, 76).

The poems of Adrienne Rich's third stage are like those of the second in that they continue to focus on the outsider, the person spurned by patriarchy. The difference in the latest volumes of Rich's poetry is that the category of the dispossessed has widened. Rich no longer focuses on the dispossession of women by men and of lesbians in particular by all patriarchal society; she is now interested to speak for any and all disadvantaged people. The more recent poetry is noticeably politically correct, often losing personal focus and vitality in an effort to speak universally. At the same time, Rich's relation to her now-dead father plays an important role in this stage. In a 1982 essay, Rich grapples with her choice of identifying herself as a Jew and thus with her father rather than her Christian mother (1986a, 100). Jews, of course, are the archetypal outsiders in Western history and culture. Rich's adult discovery of her Jewishness, like her adult discovery of her lesbianism, is consistent with her poetic and political concerns; in both cases, she identifies herself with the dispossessed in opposition to the prevailing norms of patriarchal culture. At first, being a Jew was (much like her marriage to a Jew) both an identification with her father and a separation from him, in that he chose not to acknowledge his Jewish background. Rich embraced what her father possessed but denied; she found, however, that

within Judaism patriarchal values reigned (1986a, 122), a realization
that leads eventually to a different vision of her nonobserving father.

In her ecumenical embrace of all the dispossessed in her poems
of stage three, Rich begins to see her father as a victim, as an outsider, more than as one of the males privileged in patriarchy. His
very desire to be acceptable to the accepted during the atrocities of
World War II begins to speak to her as evidence of his outsider
status. Her anger at her father has centered on his power over her
identity and on his denial of his own heritage, but Rich is now able
to see even these qualities as responses to fears of dispossession.
Rich never quite assimilates her father into her own identity, as
Sharon Olds will do later, but in this latter stage of her career, he
certainly leaves the rank of the enemy and joins the rank of those
meriting sympathy. And with this elevation of her father, Rich is also
able to recognize elements deserving empathy in nearly everyone.
Thus Rich argues for the necessity of learning to say "we" after say-
ing "I" (1986a, 224), and she is willing even to question the politics
of feminism:

> Is there a connection between . . . the Cold War mentality, the attribu-
> tion of all our problems to an external enemy—and a form of feminism
> so focussed on male evil and female victimization that it, too, allows for
> no differences among women, men, places, times, culture, conditions,
> classes, movements? (221)

In the early 1980s, Rich published a chapbook entitled "Sources,"
which has since been incorporated as the first part of the volume
Your Native Land, Your Life. Both these works are of great importance
in the study of the poet's relation to her father. It is in "Sources"
that Rich at last speaks to her dead father with empathy, person to
person and equal to equal. Notably, however, she does not do this
in verse. The two sections of the long poem that address him are in
prose, as is the section that addresses her dead husband and the
final section of the poem; the rest of the twenty-four-part work is in
verse. In section VII of "Sources," Rich, a woman in her mid-fifties,
is able to summarize with great clarity the history of her relationship
with her father. She speaks of the obsessive preoccupation with an
authoritarian father, of her role as oldest child needing to carry out
the son's role of supplanting the father. She admits to confusing the
father for a while with larger issues of patriarchy and her final recognition of the vulnerable man. And she speaks of being able finally to

face him as an equal because she has developed her own female identity (1986b, 9). Rich implies at the end of this passage that it is because she has been able to struggle against her father and gain power as a woman over him that she is able to empathize with him. That is, equality follows a swing of the power pendulum to the other side. Rich chooses this pairing of power and female identity (which perhaps represents her reunion with her father) to end "Sources" (27). The condensed psychological autobiography of section VII is impressive in its honesty, but it remains rational explanation in prose; there is no poetic, symbolic demonstration of empathy for self and father here. In fact, the poetic sections of "Sources" often present yet again the old imagery of the daughter's suffering (see especially the end of section XIII).

However, Rich tries to convert this persistent image of early victimization into the origin of her adult mission. Section XX evolves from depicting the child at the father's desk, writing poems by command, to the woman empowered to alter the rules of history (23). Her mission finds clearest expression in section XXII, in the final words she addresses to her husband, the man who killed himself after their marriage ended. Rich speaks of making a new world, in which all suffering people, such as her husband, can be at home (25). Father and husband, primary symbols of the patriarchy, are recast in "Sources" as victims needing the assistance of outsiders, who are in turn redefined as survivors of patriarchy.

The patriarchal world is turned nearly upside down in "Sources," and many of the poems in the following two parts of *Your Native Land, Your Life* carry out this new perspective. This poetry acknowledges Rich's sense of living as a strong being in her own world, no longer a victim or misfit; this volume, by allusion as well as by subject matter, corrects the wishful outsider mentality of the early poem "By No Means Native." Centrally situated within her own world as a true native and not the alien object of male exchange that Lévi-Strauss has envisioned, Rich can now look for how strength may follow weakness, how social responsibility may follow from the experience of victimage. There is much less projection of evil onto males and a much greater willingness to question the experiences of women in these later poems. The world is portrayed more realistically in shades of gray. When women die in these poems, it is not at the hands of brutal men but as a result of disease or other natural causes. *Your Native Land, Your Life* is a volume of fewer assertions and more questions, looking for possible answers to complex problems.

In "Virginia 1906" (1986b, 41–43), Rich's persona cringes at one woman's use of past abuse to justify her asocial innocence and her escapist insistence on powerlessness. Rich wants to find the victim's power, to convert her passive power of victimage into an active power of social action, to make her responsible for her own life and to society. The female subject in this poem keeps herself safely apart from any social identity, by remaining the damaged one. The "you" that appears in the title and poems of *Your Native Land, Your Life*, on the other hand, is a strong self who knows her centrality in her own life but also knows her connection to others. She is both self-aware and socially responsible, an agent of social change (46)

Rich explains much of her evolution from victim to agent of social change when she asserts that women have had to experience the extremes in order to continue to grow (Rich 1986b, 54). Sexton and Plath represent one extreme, the clinging to a victimized compliance with patriarchy, and the Rich of stage two represents the opposite extreme, the projection of all wrongdoing onto all men and the temporary alienation of women from men that is necessary to achieve balance. Mary Daly explained at the time the need for such countermeasures by reasoning that "creative justice" (1973, 173), akin to poetic justice, is needed: "What we [women] are 'seizing' and 'usurping' is that which is rightfully and ontologically ours—our own identity that was robbed from us and the power to externalize this in a new naming of reality" (164).

In her most recent volumes, from *Your Native Land, Your Life* on, Rich seeks a balance of perspectives, but Sharon Olds will begin on this middle path and move further along than Rich can at the end of her career. Rich learns from Sexton and Plath the need for a differently conceived world, and hands it on to Olds. Rich is the crucial turning point in the woman poet's process of imagining incest with the father, not just as everlasting suffering for the daughter but also as a source of growing strength and self-knowledge by taking on some of the father's power, much as Jung has envisioned it in the incest quest. Rich's courageous explorations of woman's relations with the father and patriarchy allow her to attain a greater wholeness of self, an incorporation of positive male values into her sense of identity. She thus bypasses what Rubin identifies as the great harm of heterosexuality to all people:

> The division of the sexes has the effect of repressing some of the personality characteristics of virtually everyone, men and women. The same so-

cial system which oppresses women in its relations of exchange, oppresses everyone in its insistence upon a rigid division of personality. (1975, 180)

In setting herself against her father and the fathers of society, Rich allows herself to incorporate many of their privileges, including the most important capacity to regard oneself as a desiring, willing subject with enough power to pursue and often attain what is wanted. In this way, Rich reorders the values of society, at least for herself and within the realm of poetry she controls.

Thus, the social song the poet listens to changes from the father's assertion that he knows his daughter better than she knows herself (1993a, 227) to the chorus of mothers and fathers, of all people (1986b, 67), which seems to arise from the nonincestuous society that Herman has envisioned, in which mothers and fathers, men and women, have equal power. Within such a liberated society, Rich can admit even that her father's compassion and force of expression were at times greater than her own. In a poem in which father and daughter meet a beggar, the daughter recoils but the father gives him money and speaks empathically about him (1986b, 69). This moving image suggests the poet has become aware of her father's suffering, which enables his imaginative compassion for the beggar—a state of enlightenment Rich also now comprehends. The final image of her father Rich presents in *Your Native Land, Your Life* is not that of a tyrant but of an other, evoking compassion in himself, speaking of his loneliness (1986b, 96). This is an ambivalent image. It certainly calls for compassion, but the last line is a bit too close to what an incestuous father might say to lure his daughter closer and trap her in service to him again. Lynda Boose has compared such a scenario to the aged Oedipus's expectations of service from his daughter Antigone: "an adult reversion to infantile dependency and a state of helplessness to which women—and, in particular, daughters—are expected to respond" (1989, 41). To this father Rich shows respect, empathy, but also diffidence: she does not approach him; there is no closer union than this. Rich has incorporated many of her father's social powers into her own self-image, so she does not need nor wish for a closer, physical union with him. She is no longer vulnerable to incest but has achieved the integrity of a goddess-self, identified by Jung as the goal of the incest quest.

The poetry that follows *Your Native Land, Your Life*, however, wanders away from the theme of the daughter's relations with her father. Perhaps Rich has resolved that issue in her own life; perhaps her concern for all the dispossessed makes such personal considerations less suitable for poetic exploration. The poems in these volumes are much more abstract and oracular in their attempt to speak universally and thus also much flatter in emotional tone than previous volumes. What is of interest is Rich's new attention to spiritual themes. In *Time's Power,* she alludes to the Old Testament stories (as Olds does also), and the final section of the final poem seems to be a questioning of God and Rich's relation to that presence (1989, 54). Rich's resolution of her relation with her father, her new ability to humanize him, to reduce him from Father to father, may well lead her back to considerations of the Father-figure that Christians and Jews have projected as God. Anne Sexton was also concerned at the end of her life to explore God in her poetry, but her image of God remained an inflation of the powerful father-figure she was never able to separate from. Her later poems in a sense prepare for her death by imagining a Father-God awaiting her arrival; they continue to hope for that incestuous union. Rich's godly presence, without name or sexual identity, if ever developed as a theme in poems to come, may open new images of the relation of the very vulnerable human being to the ideal parental figure he or she imagines, images of a relationship not incestuous in a negative sense but whole and transcendent.

What Rich has conceived of as a womanly union of love and power is being revived in recent years in the evolving image of the Goddess, who provides a female embodiment of power equal to the male Judeo-Christian God and thus protects women from subservience to that most patriarchal Father. With such a beneficent maternal image of power in mind, some of Sappho's words seem eerily to anticipate hopes carried by many women today for a healing return by all women and men to a transcendent mother goddess: ". . . to wish for a part of the past / Once shared is better . . . / Than that we forget" (1991, 84).

4

Sharon Olds and the Taming
of the Patriarch

SHARON OLDS'S RELATIONSHIP WITH HER POETIC FATHER IS RADICALLY different from the relationships explored by Sexton, Plath, and Rich. Where Sexton and Plath explore a compromising and harmful relationship and Rich separates from an enemy before finding a fellow outsider, Olds tames the father by remaking him into what she needs. Patricia Yaeger clarifies the new vision Olds presents and its importance in women's evolution.

> Olds talks about the father as a body—and only as a body. This kind of literary speech about the father is extraordinary; it seems to me almost unprecedented. We need to foreground Olds's choice of the father's body as poetic subject because most critical and philosophical discourse about the father evades the body altogether; it is obsessed with a father who is bodiless—who stands for the Law, for the Idea, for the Symbolic. (Yaeger 1989, 80).

Olds's embodied father thus counters Lacan's symbolic Father and the law against incest he enforces. Likewise, Olds's persona benefits from a partial breakdown of the incest taboo with the embodied father she imagines.

The poem "My Father's Breasts" introduces this embodied father:

> . . . I placed my cheek—once,
> perhaps—upon their firm shape.
>
> . . . .
> At most
> once—yet when I think of my father
> I think of his breasts, my head resting
> on his fragrant chest, as if I had spent

hours, years, in that smell of black pepper and
turned earth. (1984, 43)

What a nurturing, maternal image of the father! Yet at first, at least
in "My Father's Breasts," this physical father-imago may seem a bit
frightening, for it recalls Kavaler-Adler's warning about the power
of the maternal father and his likelihood to become the demon-
lover or Terrible Father (as discussed in chapter 2). Such a physically
seductive father-imago is what Sexton and Plath yield to and what
Rich distances herself from. Rich avoids consumption by the Terrible Father at first by identifying him in purely masculine terms of
power and then seeking love and nurture only from women, mortal
manifestations of the Good Mother. Phyllis Chesler and others have
discussed the need women have for maternal nurturing if they are
to become fully realized social beings, like men, while at the same
time confronting the frustrating reality that women are socialized to
be mothers to men, and thus lack mothering themselves or have to
provide it for themselves, which reduces their social energies. The
male has the support of mother/wife/muse in his social or creative
efforts; why should the female not have similar support from a
father/husband/muse? This seems to be the question Olds poses in
her poetry, with special reference to the father—how can the traditionally distant and neglectful or demanding father serve as a creatively nurturing muse?

Olds pursues an intimate relationship with her poetic father but
does not lose herself in it; she finds a middle ground between the
desires of Sexton and Plath and the fears of Rich. A closer look at
"My Father's Breasts" shows how. Most importantly, her contact with
her father's breasts is an imagined event. Olds takes care to qualify
that her act of laying her head on his breasts took place "once, perhaps . . . At most / once"—quite possibly never at all. Nonetheless,
the image is always accessible, as the ideal mother is and the real
father usually is not. Notable as well is that Olds depicts only the
breasts and blocks out other parts of the father not so desirable at
the moment. The image is tailored to fill certain needs and to screen
out contradictory experiences. Finally, this act of intimacy occurs at
the daughter's choice. It is available to her and not imposed on her;
the father lacks an intruding will of his own. This is a nurturing
father-imago that exists within Olds's imagination. It is an image of
a father-muse—noninvasive, supportive, maternal, from which Olds
can grow, like a plant from "turned earth." Many other poems in

Olds's canon establish that the actual father was not nurturing or supportive but rather cold, distant, and abusive. What Olds does in this poem and many others is to convert a punitive and living reality into an image that nurtures her creative growth, an image that is often openly incestuous in its depiction of physical intimacies with the father-imago. She often applies images to the father that are traditionally associated with women by men, such as the plowed earth in this poem. When the father-imago becomes receptive rather than intrusive, he is available for the daughter's creative and purposive contact. In feminizing her father-imago, Olds in turn assumes for herself certain masculine qualities of will, ambition, and self-realization. Sharon Olds is a conscious and purposeful rule-breaker in the quest for a good-enough father.

Interestingly, Olds's poetic process of taming the father, making him accessible to her needs and desires by way of symbolic incestuous contact, parallels many aspects of the Gnostic tales of the goddess Sophia. Early on in Judeo-Christian history, Sophia (Greek for wisdom) was a spirit, thought to be the first creation and equal companion of God. Sophia was the precursor of the Holy Spirit, who gave form to the original chaos and impregnated Mary with the Word of God; she was the caring intermediary between God and creation. But as Christianity grew in strength as a patriarchal political power, this female spiritual being of great power was systematically denied and her powers divided among other religious beings not so threatening to the patriarchal agenda, among them the Holy Spirit, Christ, and Mary (Engelsman 1979, 95 ff.). Sophia's fate is thus not unlike Sappho's diffusion among succeeding male poets. Sophia persists today in parts of the Old Testament and the biblical Apocrypha as a mostly depersonified value of Wisdom; in the Gnostic gospels discovered only some fifty years ago (Pagels 1989); in the writings of early Christian fathers hostile to Gnostic accounts of her; in the writings of certain thinkers, like C. G. Jung, concerned to revive a feminine spiritual complement to God; and in a widespread contemporary cultural movement to resurrect and understand what is loosely termed the "Goddess" figure.

The patriarchal Western religions today tend to portray what is left of Sophia in terms of their own cultural conceptions of women in general, much as male poets have done with Sappho. In the Old Testament and the Apocrypha, Sophia as Wisdom is often handmaiden to God or mother/wife to mankind. One verse from the Apocryphal book of Ecclesiasticus, or the Wisdom of Jesus Son of

Sirach, best sums up the patriarchal image of Sophia as an incestuous fantasy—the male's ideal dream of a mother/wife companion: "She will come to meet him like a mother, / and like a young bride she will welcome him" (Metzger and Murphy, 1991, 15:2). In these terms, Sophia fares not much better than Electra; she is presented as the compliant woman in a patriarchal culture. But in the last century, certain intellectuals, most notable the psychoanalyst Carl Jung and the Russian mystic Nicholas Solov'ev, have observed that Sophia represents a necessary complement to the patriarchal Christian God: the feminine embodiment of patience, wisdom, and empathy to counter the Old Testament God's rather tyrannical sense of rules and justice. The Jungian analyst Erich Neumann has put it this way: "Sophia is living and near, a godhead that can always be summoned and is always ready to intervene, and not a deity living inaccessible to man in numinous and alienated seclusion" (1963, 331). And the many people, women in particular, who have become involved in the cultural resurrection of the Goddess at the turn of the millennium seem intuitively to recognize that the patriarchal Judeo-Christian God represents too narrow a conception of divinity for today's culture and that the divine female counterpart must be revived and reintegrated for religion to reorient itself to the "full human dignity of women" (Christ and Plaskow 1979, 1).

The Gnostic gospels, which were written soon after Christ and posed an alternative to the more patriarchal Christian writings that have become doctrine, provide a traditional background for Sophia as a strong spiritual figure in her own right. They constitute the story the early church fathers suppressed. The Gnostic story of Sophia is complex and central to the creation myth itself; without Sophia in Gnostic theology, there would be no creation or redemption. She is the bridge or intermediary between spiritual and physical realms, and precursor to Christ and the Holy Spirit, who come into existence only because of her actions. Instead of putting forth an eternal, perfected, static goddess/handmaiden dedicated to helping mankind, the Gnostic story of creation presents a dynamic psychological portrait of Sophia. She is emotional and ambitious, and she acts on her own desires. We see her desire, act, fall, and achieve redemption, and we see it from her perspective. Most crucially, all her acts proceed initially from her desire for an incestuous union with the Father, Bythos, the supreme creator. In short, Sophia's story is the archetypal incest myth from the daughter's perspective, which informs the incest complex observed by Freud and Jung and perhaps underlies the predominance of recovered memories of incest today.

The teachings of the Gnostic scholar Valentinus, which constitute the most complete account of Sophia's story, are preserved only in the writings of two orthodox Christian fathers, Irenaeus and Hippolytus, who recorded them in order to brand them as heresies and refute them. Despite his own antagonism, Irenaeus presents Sophia's complex story with clarity. Sophia is the last-conceived of a great spiritual family of Aeons, and as the last she seems to have no creative role, to be just the end of the line. Finding this condition lacking, she in turn conceives the impulse of reuniting herself with the first Father of them all, Bythos (or Abyss), which might generously be seen as an impulse toward closing the circle of spirits, an honorable act of incest. Irenaeus, however, not unlike cultural fathers today in their responses to recovered memories, condemns Sophia's behavior as lamentably ambitious, because it strays from what is expected of her role as last daughter and because of its results.

> . . . [T]his degenerate Aeon [Sophia] . . . acted under a pretence of love, but was in reality influenced by temerity, because she had not, like Nous [the first-conceived, male spirit after the Father], enjoyed communion with the perfect Father. This passion . . . consisted in a desire to search into the nature of the Father; for she wished . . . to comprehend his greatness. . . . [T]here was danger lest she should at last have been absorbed by his sweetness, and resolved into his absolute essence, unless she had met with that Power which supports all things, and preserves them outside of the unspeakable greatness [Horos]. . . . [T]hen, having with difficulty been brought back to herself, she was convinced that the Father is incomprehensible, and so laid aside her original design, along with that passion which had arisen within her from the overwhelming influence of her admiration. (Irenaeus 1953, 317)

Note here the striking similarity to Jung's scenario of the incest quest as a regression toward the mother (or father) which might end in the individual's absorption into her as Terrible Mother (or him as Terrible Father), except that the incest taboo prevents that union, leading the child to create, it is hoped, a symbolic union instead. The Gnostic story of Sophia is an early version of the daughter's desire for incestuous union with the father, and of the dangerous conditions the individual on this quest must confront. What is most interesting is that the Gnostics considered the power of the incest desire in the daughter as crucial to creation. Because Sophia does find a way to unite symbolically with her father through acts of creation, her desire may be seen as heroic, the first and thus archetypal version for women of the process Jung has called individuation. In the Gnostic story, the other Aeons act to counter Sophia's action and to bring her back into her place in their preestablished order. Sophia is the only Aeon to break out of the static perfection of this spiritual realm and bring about a process of creation, in which spirit merges with matter. That is, she breaks out of the closed system with her desire and opens it to growth and change. Horos (an apparent embodiment of the incest taboo in this tale) reunites Sophia with the other Aeons and restores her to her original place, but he is able to do this only by projecting her desire for union with her father outside of the spiritual realm. Sophia's desire thus takes on its own life in a lower realm of matter; it is apparently too strong to be extinguished and must find its own form elsewhere.

According to the Gnostic story, after Sophia is reclaimed in the spiritual realm and her inadmissible desire projected outward, another pair of Aeons is created (Christ and the Holy Spirit) to assuage and appease the original spirits in order that no further transgressions like Sophia's take place. Then Christ gives form to Sophia's desire in the lower realm out of pity for its formless condition; this being becomes Achamoth, or the material form of Sophia. Achamoth then repeats Sophia's original desire for the Father and despairs when Christ (Logos) leaves her. She is restrained by Horos again, and her passions give rise to the creation of the material world (Irenaeus 1953, 320–21). With Achamoth, as with Sophia originally and with many women artists today, creation follows abandonment by the father to a state of repressive limitations, and represents the woman's effort to mitigate the futility and frustration of that situation. This Gnostic story of creation most notably establishes female emotions as the primary elements of creation, and not male rationality or language. Male form is brought to bear only in response to the female's rebellion against the status quo. The father responds (indirectly) to his daughter only when the daughter refuses her subordinate position and desires union. It is the daughter's refusal that ultimately brings about an empathic male response in Christ—a response that seems to emanate not just from male reason and perfection but also from female emotion (pity). And the final consummation envisioned by the Gnostics is of a unification of spiri-

tual and material worlds that comes about only because of the rebellious actions of Sophia and her lower projection, Achamoth.

> When all the seed shall have come to perfection, . . . then . . . Achamoth
> shall . . . enter in within the Pleroma [spiritual realm], and shall receive
> as her spouse the Saviour, who sprang from all the Aeons, that thus a
> conjunction may be formed between the Saviour and Sophia, that is,
> Achamoth. These, then, are the bridegroom and bride. . . . Sophia . . .
> having lost her enthymesis [desire] afterwards recovered it, on all things
> being purified by the advent of the Saviour. (Irenaeus 1953, 325–28)

Iranaeus's summary is illuminating. It would seem that it is
Christ's purifying influence that brings about the unification of
spirit and matter, but Irenaeus makes clear that the Gnostics saw
that it was Sophia's original passion for unification with the Father
(her "enthymesis") that is finally consummated in her union with
Christ—the union not only of spiritual and material realms but also
of male and female principles. The incest desire is ultimately and
paradoxically the heretical passion that brings about the highest
consummation. Sophia could not achieve union with the Father,
who would have consumed her, but her incestuous desire carries out
a process of creation that culminates in her union with a male heir
of the Father, who is accessible because he already combines some
elements of the female with his male being, having come into being
as a result of her desire. That is, Sophia's desire for her father brings
about not only a more whole spiritual being in Christ, but also her
own union with this more complete being. Both Sophia and Christ
exhibit masculine and feminine qualities and then merge those
qualities further in their union. Where her father, as original and
originating Patriarch, would have annihilated Sophia if she had per-
sisted in desiring him, Christ, as a modification of the father by way
of her desire, completes her and all spiritual and material creation
in his union with her. In Jung's terms, consumption by the Terrible
Father has been avoided, and Sophia has found her own more complete self in union with the Good Father that she has caused to come
into being in response to her desires. This might be called the middle way of Sophia—not complicity with the patriarchy (like Electra)
nor the alienation of separatist social thought or action (like Sappho), but a creative combination of the two.
    The Gnostic story of Sophia disproves Jung's lament: "Unfortu-
nately, our Western mind . . . has never yet devised a concept, nor

even a name, for the *union of opposites through the middle path,* that most fundamental item of inward experience" (Jung 1980, 7:205). Perhaps Jung could not see this potential in Sophia because he assumed the quest to be male-generated (see, for instance, his *Answer to Job* [Jung 1980, 11]), whereas Mary Daly has made clear that only a female quest can succeed in overcoming the limitations of patriarchy (1973, 72 ff.), since only a woman as outsider has the need and desire to move beyond the system. What the Gnostic story of Sophia shows that seems so relevant to the role of women, especially creative women today, is that Sophia needs to force her intuitive, partly unconscious desire onto a patriarchy that finds it disturbing and offensive. She must act out a process that seems within her own sphere of being an ungrateful and perhaps even insane rebellion. But the persistence of her desire leads ultimately to a fuller and more dynamic creation, and to a unity between different parts of the whole that was not possible within the closed system in which she began her quest. At the end of her story, Sophia is no longer the barred and impotent daughter but a full woman: daughter and mother, wife, lover, creator. The Gnostic story of Sophia shows us what the story of Eve, one of her daughters, also may show us—that the disobedient and desiring daughter is the crucial element in creation and evolution beyond patriarchal stasis.

Nowhere in her poetry does Sharon Olds show any awareness of the Gnostic story of Sophia, but her poetry does attempt to achieve something similar to Sophia's quest, albeit on a more personal scale. In the course of her first four volumes of poetry, Olds achieves a reconceived relation with the father not unlike Sophia's: an open expression of desire for union with the father, not shirking its incestuous connotations; a materialization and even to some extent a feminization of the remote and rejecting father-figure (the father with breasts, not a chest); and a union of what is most essential to her in that father with herself. The father-daughter relationship is one of Olds's primary themes throughout her poetry, but particularly in her fourth volume, *The Father.* Despite the formality of the title, this book of poems works through the poet's personal relationship with her father as he dies. However, Olds's poems as a group also show an awareness of the Father as a cultural symbol of authority and inaccessibility, like Sophia's father, Bythos. *The Father* thus achieves a balanced vision of the personal and cultural father-figures in a daughter's life, much as Sexton's and Plath's Daddy poems do.

However, Olds is much more aware of the personal and social implications of her topic than Sexton or Plath. This is so in part because Olds is the heir of Adrienne Rich, a beneficiary of her separation from and partial reconciliation with the father. Olds is able to create a positive union with her father-imago in part because Rich has already completed the necessary prior rebellion. Rich's lesbian poetry opens the way to Olds's highly erotic heterosexual poetry, which Rich herself has praised in terms of the "undomesticated passion of the erotically alive mother" (Rich 1993c, 158). Olds writes poems of passion not just about her husband and children but also about her father. She is the only one of the four poets in this study eventually to imagine a positive, creative, spiritually incestuous relationship with her father—one fully advantageous to the poet-daughter because it is controlled by her and not harmful to the father, because it uses only the daughter's imago and not the father's social identity. Olds uses her father-imago intimately, as a muse, without fear of his penetrating control, a fear Rich never quite loses.

Olds's initial images of her father are not positive, however. Several of Olds's early poems seem to allude to Plath poems in an attempt to resolve some of the dilemmas Plath presents in her poetry. One example is "That Year," from *Satan Says* (1980, 6–7), in which Olds compares herself as a child emotionally abused by her father with the Jewish victims of the Nazis during the Holocaust, much in the mode of Plath's "Daddy" and "Lady Lazarus." However, Olds ends her poem with one crucial distinction between herself and those lost Jews: she names herself a "survivor." Where Plath opens up the parallel between tyranny in father-daughter relations and tyranny in global social relations, Olds seems to close it with an act of will and a word that preserves her own individuality. She, unlike Plath and like Rich, refuses to be a victim of the patriarchal system, and Olds finds there are words that open up alternatives to such victimage—her escape is by way of language.

Another poem from the same volume also develops the parallel of personal life and social experiences during World War II. Olds declares: "I would be / for myself, then, an enemy / to all who do not wish me to rise" ("The Rising Daughter," Olds 1980, 19). Unlike Plath's declaration of transcendence over men at the end of "Lady Lazarus," Olds's transcendence does not depend on consuming her enemies. Her independence by way of language frees her of them, while Plath's bid for independence actually ties her, like Electra, closer to them. And where Rich suspects that even language itself supports patriarchal structures, Olds finds resources within the language to strengthen herself. Olds appropriates words for her own needs, shaking a word like "survivor" or "enemy" free of its larger social context and situating it within her personal experience. Where Plath's persona identifies almost completely with certain elements of historical experience, even to the point of believing herself a Jew in "Daddy," Olds uses language to separate and free herself from complicity in tyrannical contexts.

Olds's self-conscious exploration of the troubled relations between father and daughter is also aided by an awareness of psychoanalytic insights, which are more generally available to the culture Olds inhabits today than they were to the culture Sexton and Plath wrote in, some thirty years before. In fact, Olds's poetic speaker makes clear that she is not only aware of her status as a survivor of an abusive family life, but also that she is the wife of a psychiatrist (see "I Am the Shrink's Wife," Olds 1980, 25–26). If, as Leonard Shengold has stated, therapy for survivors of childhood abuse aims to "get rid of the invading intra-psychic monster—that is, to undo or at least ameliorate the damaging identification with the soul-destroying parent" (1989, 6), the Terrible Father in the case of these poets, then much of Olds's poetry works through the therapeutic task of converting the soul-destroying parent to a soul-nurturing imago. The poetry seems at times almost a self-conscious demonstration of that task. All the same, the necessity of rebellion seems to come a bit reluctantly to Olds at first. Her first volume, *Satan Says* (1980), is conscious of this need but also cautious. In "Satan Says" (3–4), the first poem of the volume, Olds's persona is locked in a casket-like box, from which Satan offers her a conditional escape: "*Say: the father's cock, the mother's / cunt,* says Satan, *I'll get you out. . . .*" At first Olds's speaker responds as instructed, and the box begins to open, but when she sees she must exit through Satan's mouth, she recalls her love for her parents and resists Satan's persuasions. This poem introduces the paradoxical themes of Olds's poetry, which will be met with in the succeeding volumes as well.

In truth, Olds nearly always maintains an awareness of love for her parents that transcends her anger and hurt, but the reduction of parental figures to physical parts, sexual parts in particular (like her father's breasts)—the reduction of the parents to mere physical begetters and sustainers of Olds herself—becomes the hallmark of her therapeutic poetry. It is not that she ever forgets or rejects the emotional ties to her parents, but she also progresses by recasting her parents, her father in particular, in physical terms. Part of the power of this move lies with reimagining the father not as social authority figure only, the unreachable phallic power like Sophia's Father, but as a fragile and fallible individual physical being, more like the speaker herself or like the descendent of the Father, Jesus, who also lived and died on this earth. "Satan Says" thus introduces two themes that Olds will develop in tandem throughout the rest of her poetry: the love for her parents, especially for her father (which draws her to them much as Sophia was drawn toward her Father), and the need to rebel against them, again especially the father, so as not to be consumed within their system (as Sophia's desire opened up her original family system). At first in this volume, Satan embodies the need to rebel and tempts the Electral daughter, as in the traditional story of Eve, but soon enough Olds's speaker accepts her own instinct to rebel and acts on it in a measured way, rejecting her parents partially but not totally.

The structure of *Satan Says* stages the need to rebel in its four parts: Daughter, Woman, Mother, and Journey. If, indeed, a journey is to be made through these three female roles and perhaps beyond, the first, crucial role of daughter has to be understood, resolved, and transcended. In a certain sense, as implied in "Satan Says," Sharon Olds remains the Electral daughter, the compliant female within the patriarchal system. She shows no persistent desire to change the system itself, as Rich does; Olds rather desires to make the system more congenial to herself. When the system seems to stifle her, she recalls the priority of her love for the individuals in it. Rebellion does not mean, for her, repeating the father's mistake of deserting and harming loved ones.

> . . . I am so tired of the women doing dishes
> and how smart the men are, and how I want to
> bite their mouths and feel their hard cocks against me.
>
> . . . .
> . . . I am tired of the children,
> I am tired of the laundry. I want to be great.
>
> . . . .
> . . . The only way out is through
> fire, and I do not want a single
> hair of a single head singed. (30)

The structure of this volume and the poems throughout her canon affirm quite emphatically that Olds wants to evolve through the usual development of daughter, woman, wife, mother. She may have been an unhappy daughter, but she finds a way to affirm her daughterhood and her father. She may be the shrink's wife, but she affirms her experience as such. Olds is fully committed to the normal heterosexual, monogamous role assigned to women in a patriarchy; she celebrates it and defines herself by it. Certainly, she exposes the sexual side of this role to a greater extent than is usually acceptable, but this is part of her method of making the role itself fuller and more congenial to her needs, rather than breaking out of the system. Sophia, similarly, may have broken out of the system, but ultimately her actions expanded and affirmed it.

The poem following "Satan Says," "Love Fossil" (1980, 5), immediately opens the wound inflicted by the father on the daughter. The prehistoric imagery captures nicely not only the realm of a young girl's imagination in loving her father, but also the paradox of that love: that getting your father to respond to your love is about as likely as finding a living carnivorous dinosaur to eat you up—and about as smart too.

> I did not understand his doom or my taste for the big
>   dangerous body.
> I flashed my animal sides, and he was
> vegetarian to the end.

The frustration of the incest taboo, which seems to dictate (to this father, as to so many others) not only that the father not touch his daughter in a sexual manner but that he not respond to her emotionally, is resolved by Olds in an interesting way: "He taught me to love / what was stuck, what couldn't help itself, / what went down mute into time like tar, like anger. . . ." Identifying with the elusive father as a method of achieving some contact with him is a common response in daughters, but usually this response leads to a suppression of the daughter's desire and ambition, in common with her father's obvious lack of desire and ambition for her, as Gayle Rubin shows in her analysis of the Oedipal complex in girls. Olds's apparent ability to present the wound and the cure almost simultaneously is stunning. How is it that she can love the very characteristics in her father that have wounded and reduced her, without being entrapped in that wound, and still achieve a full and free celebration of her self?

Some clues may be found in the poem of greatest pain in *Satan Says*, "Reading You" (1980, 70). Olds's language is often on the verge of shocking, and her poetic style usually breaks even the very lax formal expectations of contemporary poetry. The poem uses these transgressions to carry in image and style the chaos of the daughter's emotional wound, which is not yet fully healed.

> . . . Man, male, his [father's] cock that I have loved
> beyond the others, beyond goodness, so far beyond
> pleasure I have loved his hatred, coldness,
> indifference, solid blackness
>
> . . . .
>
> The chest, breasts, bathing suit—half
> me, half mine! Never mine, nothing.
>
> . . . .
>
> cock promised and never given
> that I would strip my skin for. . . .

"Reading You" is dedicated to a fellow writer, male, and it shows that in reading his words Olds finds some relief and consolation, as if hearing her father speak. One of Olds's methods of transcending her father's limitations and their potential reduction of her while also accepting them and avoiding her own demise, is to speak out of the physical presence that her father was for her, to give voice to a man who would not and could not speak to her or for her when she needed such affirmation. At first, in "Reading You," Olds hears her father's voice in the words of another male poet, but soon she will learn to speak her father for herself. In learning this ventriloquy (reminiscent of male poets speaking through Sappho), Olds also learns empathy and overcomes her father's limitations by her own talents. And, importantly, Olds reclaims her father's body, sex and all, as part of her own identity, thus transforming the separate, un-reachable, denying Terrible Father into an agent of her own power, the internal Good Father. She usurps the traditional male poetic role of desiring subject and recasts her father as loved object.

In "The Sisters of Sexual Treasure" (1980, 24), Olds records the particular delight she and her sister found in escaping their father's negation of them through their initiation in sex:

> . . . The men's bodies
> were like our father's body!
>
> . . . .
>
> we could have him there, the steep forbidden

> buttocks, backs of the knees, the cock
> in our mouth, ah the cock in our mouth. . . .

The sisters' desire for the father's penis, "promised and never given," yields to the availability of the penises of other men, as the Oedipally socialized daughters pass from forbidden father to available father-surrogates. Direct, literal incest is thus appropriately avoided, but Olds does not shrink from insisting on the emotional incest that persists. Part of the joy of heterosexual sex for Olds is the symbolic fulfillment of the incest desire it provides. "The cock in our mouth" is for Olds an image of empowerment, not a suppression or silencing, because she takes it in voluntarily and does not conceive of it as being forced on her. If the penis/phallus symbolizes social power, then certainly it is typically withheld from women by men and not forced on them. Yet like Sophia, Olds does not insist on the defamation of her father or entirely renounce the system; she seeks and finds her own means of fulfillment within that system, by opening it up to further growth. The system is opened in Olds's case by her insistence on the acceptance and even celebration of the daughter's incestuous desire for her father, the strongest psychological taboo in a patriarchy. That limit dissolved, at least in psychological or symbolic terms, Olds is free to sing from the acknowledged depths of her own desire.

Olds's rebellious action is symbolic, verbal. She will seize the phallus, the power of the male in a patriarchal system, but in her poetry and not through political action. Language is the locus of power for Olds, as she reveals in a touching poem in which she explores her poetic kinship with Walt Whitman, entitled "Nurse Whitman" (1980, 13). Olds develops a parallel between Whitman's reparative attentions to Civil War casualties and her own healing verbal focus on her father.

> . . . You bathe the forehead, you bathe the lip, the cock,
> as I touch my father, as if the language
> were a form of life.
> .   .   .   .
> We lean down, our pointed breasts
> heavy as plummets with fresh spermy milk—
> we conceive, Walt, with the men we love, thus, now,
> we bring to fruit.

Poetry is the language of compassion for Olds, as for Whitman—the language of community, of connection and comprehension. Not only does it give voice to the victims of society and thus integrate them, but it creates a union in the poet her/himself of male and female values and attributes. This inclusive kind of poetry combines milk and sperm, comforting nourishment and enabling power, creating a greater self, at least in verse. As with the union of Jesus and Sophia as androgynous characters at the culmination of the Gnostic story of creation, Olds conceives of herself and Whitman working poetically and androgynously to reunite themselves and the nation. Again, all this may not be externally realizable in society, but it is available internally and in the symbolic enactment of desire in poetry.

One result of Olds's assuming some of the phallic power of the father is, paradoxically, empathy for her father as another victim of the system of patriarchy, even more a victim than she herself—a consequence much like the sympathy Rich develops for her father after unseating him as a potential threat in her life. In several poems from her second and third volumes, *The Dead and the Living* and *The Gold Cell,* Olds identifies elements of the patriarchy, including her own paternal grandfather and her father's employer, that have victimized her father (see "The Guild" and "The Victims," Olds 1984, 12, 34.) The tables are turned as the daughter refuses victimage, transcends the normal limitations of her role in a patriarchy, and bestows sympathy on her father for his plight. The phallus seems to be more the daughter's than the father's at this point.

Unlike Plath and Sexton, Olds learns not to portray herself as victim. But more importantly she comes to pity the perpetrators as victims in their own right, much as Rich turns the tables on patriarchy as she installs herself as subject in her own world.

> . . . I had seen my father
> strung and mottled, mauled as if taken and
> raked by a crowd, and I of the crowd
> over his body, and how could the day be
> good after that, how could anything be good
> in such a world, I turned my back
> on happiness, at 13 I entered
> a life of mourning, of mourning for the Fascist. (1987, 26)

Plath, who never properly mourned the loss of her father and never came to know him as an individual equal to herself in the world, was as an adult unable to replace him after his death. Olds has the advantage of an adult relationship with her father, and uses it to detach herself from her father as a symbol of protection and authority, the Father, and then to pity him as a human being more fragile and broken than herself—more broken because he is less able to improvise within the patriarchal system than she is. In his role in the system, he is a "Fascist," but he is also simply a beaten man.

Once her father's victimage is pitied and her own emotional survival established, Olds is free to develop her image of the ideal father, the father needed and desired by daughters. The Terrible Father is defused through pity for the man's human weaknesses, and the Good Father, even the inspiring muse-father, can be developed symbolically in his place. In *The Dead and the Living*, Olds presents her image of "The Ideal Father" (1984, 38–39).

> When I dream you, Dad,
> .   .   .   .
> You're perfect as a textbook example.
> .   .   .   .
> Where is the one who threw up?
> .   .   .   .
> I think he is dead.
> I think the ideal father would hardly
> let such a man live. After all he has
> daughters to protect, laying his perfect
> body over their sleep all night long.

Olds revives the imagery of incest to depict the perfect father, much as Sexton tries to identify her real father by the right to incest in "The Death of the Fathers," but the incest Olds envisions is symbolic and protective—a contact of dreams, in which the father protects and promotes the well-being of his daughters. This is not an incubus who invades his daughters' bodies for his own pleasure, like Anne Sexton's dybbuk (to be discussed in the conclusion), but a motherly father, rather like the Holy Spirit brooding over creation. This ideal, spiritual father adds his powers to enhance his daughters' own potential, ensuring that their dreams be realized and not broken. This is certainly a muse image, a dream-lover carrying all the power of sexual attraction and social prohibition, which the grown Olds calls on for her own enhancement and inspiration.

As the image of the father lying over his sleeping daughters depicts the daughter's need for the father is not fully conscious. In part because the relation is physical, genetic, and in part because Olds's father was always more physically than emotionally present in her life, Olds learns to feast on his body rather than feed from his mind, as we see in "Looking at My Father" (1987, 31–32). This is another kind of incest, the daughter glutting herself on the sight of her father's body, sating her need of him as image rather than body.

> . . . I know he is not perfect but my
> body thinks his body is perfect
>
> . . . .
>
> what my
> body knows it knows, it likes to
> slip the leash of my mind and go and
> look at him, like an animal
> looking at water, then going to it and
> drinking until it has had its fill and can
> lie down and sleep.

Provocatively, this image of looking at the father as an animal looks at water and then drinks is much the same image Carl Jung uses in reference to Sophia: "the way of the soul in search of its lost father— like Sophia seeking Bythos—leads to the water, to the dark mirror that reposes at its bottom. . . . a living symbol of the dark psyche" (1980, 9:17).

Extending this image with reference to Olds, one might imagine that the unself-conscious animal would drink its fill but that the fully conscious human daughter would be arrested by her own image in the water, in the depths of her soul. The father, as muse, becomes a guide to deeper self-knowledge, a more available conscious realization of what Jung has called the animus figure in the unconscious mind:

> The animus is the deposit, as it were, of all woman's ancestral experiences of man—and not only that, he is also a creative and procreative being, not in the sense of masculine creativity, but in the sense that he brings forth something we might call . . . the spermatic word. (Jung 1980, 7:208)

The daughter with the "spermatic word," the daughter in communion with this father-figure (like Olds and Whitman with their "spermy milk") can create her own poetic world.

In the poem "Fate" (1984, 40), Olds "just gave up and became my father," or at least she accepts fully his presence inside her. She discovers it can be a positive presence that leads to her own blossoming, as if she were a tulip flower and he the bulb "impacted" in the soil. And in several poems of the later volumes, Olds quite naturally identifies herself with the very sperm that led to her conception.

> . . . I
> whipped my tail and sailed up and
> saw the egg like a trap door in the
> side of the jail and I pushed through it
> head first, my tail fell off I be-
> gan to explode in ecstasy re-
> leased. . . . (1987, 44)

This is an extraordinary image, for Olds is quite clearly identifying herself with the active, ambitious sperm, often imagined as male for those attributes, and not with the passive, female egg. Olds also identifies with the eruptive male orgasm within the female. These images explode many stereotypes of female role behavior, but why should women not identify themselves more strongly with the sperm that carried their determining sex gene than with the egg? Olds is able to defy convention because she has incorporated her father, accepting his presence as part of her, rather than seeing him as unalterably opposed to her on the basis of gender.

Even when Olds tries to imagine her mother's sexual experience in conceiving her, she imagines it as the female desiring union with the male, completing herself by uniting with the masculine attributes she admires so much in him. In "Why My Mother Made Me" (1987, 33), Olds speculates: "Maybe I am what she always wanted, / my father as a woman." Each child is a whole, the conjunction of sexual complements through desire. Why should she not celebrate her own masculine makeup, as well as her feminine identity? Olds thus finds a way to retain the phallus, rather than letting it just pass through her on its way to another privileged generation of males. This seems to be another example of how Olds is able to shape an image of the patriarchal society she lives in to benefit herself, to fill her needs and suit her desires, rather than rejecting that society out of hand. It is an inclination that goes back to the first poem of *Satan Says*, combining the need to rebel and the desire to love. This is not an unconscious, Electral compliance, but an aware, chosen, empathic action, a calculated compromise with fate, as she makes clear in "Little Things" (1987, 68).

> . . . I think I learned to
> love the little things about him [father]
> because of all the big things
> I could not love, no one could, it would be wrong to.
> . . . .
> I am doing something I learned early to do, I am
> paying attention to small beauties,
> whatever I have—as if it were our duty to
> find things to love, to bind ourselves to this world.

The Father is the first of Olds's volumes not to be divided in several parts; it appears to be a simple sequence of fifty-three poems, a record of the process of the father's death as it occurred. However, a second reading reveals that there is a central poem, both thematically and structurally. "The Dead Body" is the first poem of the volume to deal with the father as an inanimate thing; it does not even revive memories of his life, as even the poem "The Exact Moment of His Death" does. In "The Dead Body" Olds faces and must come to terms with the absolute end of her father's life and her own ongoing existence. The literal centrality of the poem suggests that this is the central, crucial experience for Olds in the volume, perhaps even in her relationship with her father—the moment at which the father loses his power as a living being and becomes a symbol in the mind of his daughter. From this point on, he is in her power; she can use him as she wishes. This is the realization that makes the volume not just a personal record of a daughter confronting her father's death, but also a much more universal exploration of the potential women carry for transforming the father-imago into an agent of nurture, the Good Father, rather than a persistent agent of limitation, the Terrible Father.

It is somewhat surprising from this perspective that the opening poem of the volume, "The Waiting" (1992, 3–4), and several other early poems present the dying father as a rather diffident god, sufficient within himself and attended by his daughter because of her desire, not his. Biblical allusions at times seem to reinforce this impression. The volume opens with the (bath)robed Father, the Patriarch on his (wing-back) throne, confidently anticipating the attentions of his daughter. As she approaches, he would

> . . . then slew his eyes up at me, without
> moving his head, and wait, the kiss

came to him, he did not go to it.
. . . .
                                        night-
watchman of matter, sitting, facing
the water—the earth without form, and void,
darkness upon the face of it, as if
waiting for his daughter.

If the beginning of this poem presents a rather deferential attitude by daughter to father, allowing him to maintain a godly demeanor, like the robed Old Testament God on his throne, the end of the poem suggests a different reality. After all, this "god" is dying, his robe a bathrobe, his presence at dawn a sign of insomnia. The last three lines of the poem paraphrase Genesis 1:2: "the earth was a formless void and darkness covered the face of the deep, while a wind from God swept over the face of the waters." The wind, or spirit, of God that moves over the water just before creation is usually taken to be the Holy Spirit, associated with Sophia. In Olds's poem, the daughter takes the place of the Holy Spirit, like Sophia being restored to her rightful place as companion of God. But it is the daughter who seems to be responsible for the emergence of light, as she rises at dawn to greet her father, and not the unmoving father himself. There is no light or form until the daughter arrives with the dawn, much as there was no creation until after Sophia began her quest to be united with her Father or until the Holy Spirit gave form to matter. The power of the Father, the Patriarch in this poem, is only potential; the phallic potency is realized by the daughter. The poem may provide an image of a patriarchal culture and religion in need of revival by the goddess figure.

A question opens here, as it does in the story of Sophia: does the daughter attend her father, waiting for his death, out of love or ambition? Is her presentation of the light a demonstration of love or power? In Olds's poetry, especially in this volume, it seems to be both. Another early poem, "The Glass" (1992, 7–8), presents the father as a god able to manufacture food from his mouth. But this food is mucous gagged up from a cancerous throat and spit into a glass. This glass becomes for Olds a new center of meaning, shifting the whole order of existence in her world away from the father and toward his death; it is the particular inanimate image of his approaching non-being.

> . . . the room seemed to turn around it [glass]
> in an orderly way, a model of the solar system
> turning around the sun,
> my father the old earth that used to
> lie at the center of the universe, now
> turning with the rest of us
> around his death. . . .

This Copernican revolution in her emotional existence liberates the daughter. The death of the father's godhood, confirmed in the evidence of his mortality, releases the powers inherent in the daughter. She will soon no longer serve him but replace him as an equal, another mortal revolving around the fact of human mortality.

In the meantime, this death, this transfer of power from father to daughter, takes work. It must be accomplished with skill and tact. The old order must be ushered out with respect so that the new can take its place without regret, in full power. This labor is presented in "The Picture I Want" (1992, 10), the image Olds would like to retain from the process.

> . . . my face as near
> to the primary tumor as a dozing baby's
> lips to the mother's breast.
>
> . . . .
>
> we are resting on each other,
> almost asleep.

Her father's death is food for Olds. In "The Picture I Want," Olds receives food and comfort, physical and spiritual nourishment from the physical proximity that nursing her father allows, but also from the reality of his death—his tumor is like a breast to her. It is as if the father were to say of his daughter what John the Baptist said of Jesus: "he must increase, but I must decrease" (John 3:30). But of course, this father would never say that of his daughter. As he dies, the father remains ensconced in the patriarchal system, highly deferential to male figures of authority (the doctors and priests in such poems as "His Terror" and "The Struggle") and nearly oblivious to his daughter's presence. Olds knows she must tactfully take her place as his successor, and that her opportunity is his death.

Not surprisingly, several early poems in this volume present images of birth in tandem with images of death. It is customarily expected that the daughter will carry her father's memory after his death, in effect giving birth to a new life for him. But the poem in which Olds considers this possibility is titled "Nullipara" (1992, 5), and in "The Pulling" (1992, 6), the concept of her father regressing into a new infancy does not reburden the daughter with pregnancy, reducing her to a servant of the patriarchy; rather, it delivers her to a new role, in that the birth is in reality a death, and she the creator of the new life form her father will assume inside of her.

> . . . I sense every inch of him [father] moving
> through me toward it [death], the way each child
> moved, slowly, down through my body,
> as if I were God.
> .   .   .   .
> as if my father could live and die
> safely inside me.

The father is surely making the transition from physical being to psychic image, and the daughter is the creator and preserver of that image, the new god. It is in this sense that the phallus of power does not necessarily pass through the woman on the way to the next generation of males. If what is valued is spiritual existence, psychic experience and not physical attributes, then the power usually attributed to the father can be arrested and retained within the creative daughter.

Olds frequently uses two sets of images to capture this process of taking in her father and retaining him. One is the imagery of food and eating, such as the daughter nursing at her father's tumor in "The Picture I Want" and the mucous as food in "The Glass." The food of the father's death is taken in, digested, literally assimilated by the daughter into herself, and it produces a revolutionary redefinition of self, an enhancement and empowerment. The other imagery is that of sex, and here again it becomes clear that symbolic incest is highly desirable, even necessary for the daughter's full self-realization. On one level, sexuality is a transfer of power for Olds. As she says in "Death and Morality" (1992, 9), the reality of her father's death is the "world where sex lives." When Olds sees her father's penis in "The Lifting" (1992, 15–16), when it is made available to her because it is no longer a protected symbol of his power but now just another appendage on a decaying body, sex indeed becomes a vehicle for the transfer of power.

> . . . If anyone had ever told me
> I would sit by him and he would pull up his nightie

and I would look at him, at his naked body,
at the thick bud of his penis in all that
dark hair, look at him
in affection and uneasy wonder
I would not have believed it. But now I can still
see the tiny snowflakes, white and
night-blue, on the cotton of the gown as it
rises the way we were promised at death it would rise,
the veils would fall from our eyes, we would know everything.

With the lifting of the veil, the mystery of the phallus is deprived of its exclusively masculine power. The daughter sees the phallus not as the iron rod of authority, as it seems to be when withheld from the daughter, but a bud that may blossom in her. In the final lines of "The Lifting," Olds is perhaps alluding to 2 Corinthians 3:15–18, on the deliverance of Christians from the patriarchal Mosaic laws by the Spirit of God.

Indeed, to this very day whenever Moses is read, a veil lies over their minds; but when one turns to the Lord, the veil is removed. Now the Lord is the Spirit, and where the Spirit of the Lord is, there is freedom. And all of us, with unveiled faces, seeing the glory of the Lord as though reflected in a mirror, are being transformed into the same image from one degree of glory to another; for this comes from the Lord, the Spirit.

What follows the demystification of patriarchal power is an equal and free access to spiritual truths. It is tempting to read this symbol of lifting the veil in terms of Jung's sense of the need to make the transition from literal, infantile ties with the parents to the "symbolic equivalent." What follows this accomplishment is spiritual rebirth through the "divine creative power" discovered in the symbolic parent (Jung 1980, 5:336).

That Olds is empowered by this lifting of the veil of patriarchal mystery is apparent in a following poem, which once again alludes to a biblical story to reinforce the spiritual magnitude of this transfer of power. In "Last Words" (1992, 23), Olds procrastinates in leaving her father's bedside until in exasperation he asks her to kiss him one final time and then be gone.

. . . and it is ending with a *kiss*—
a command for mercy, the offer of his cracked
creator lips. To plead that I leave,

my father asked me for a kiss! I would not
leave till he had done so, I will not let thee go except thou beg for it.

The daughter speaks here with the biblical voice of power that was
previously projected onto the father. The story she alludes to in the
final clause is Jacob's fight with the messenger from God. When it is
clear to the messenger that he cannot win the wrestling match with
Jacob before dawn, when he must leave, he begs to be released.
Jacob, who now has power over this heavenly being, responds, "I will
not let you go, unless you bless me" (Genesis 32:26). Jacob's endur-
ance and ambition are repaid not only with a blessing but also with
a change in his name to Israel, which witnesses to his new role as
God's representative on earth. The messenger puts it this way: "You
shall no longer be called Jacob, but Israel, for you have striven with
God and with humans, and have prevailed" (32:28). Jacob realizes,
"I have seen God face to face, and yet my life is preserved" (32:30).

Like Jacob, Olds prevails over her father by out-enduring him, by
surviving him, and she is blessed in a sense not only by his request
for a kiss but by his lifting of the veil, his revelation of the phallus,
the symbol of patriarchal authority. Olds sees this symbol face to
face, as it were, and survives. She accepts the reality of the daughter's
incest desire, which is usually hidden along with the forbidden
penis, and for this accomplishment, she is blessed and given a future
of much greater possibilities than she ever faced before as good patriarchal daughter. This is the point of psychic transition from literal
to symbolic father, from Terrible to Good Father, a transition even
Jung describes in terms that recall the story of Jacob: "he [internal
god] appears first in hostile form, as an assailant with whom the
hero has to wrestle. . . . In this manner the god manifests himself
and in this form he must be overcome" (Jung 1980, 5:337). Olds has
in effect tamed the Terrible Father with a kiss, transforming him
into the Good Father who gives her the kiss as a somewhat begrudg-
ing blessing.

It is interesting that in many poems in *The Father* Olds effects this
transformation by rewriting tales from the Bible; in doing so she establishes her own speaking voice in the position traditionally occu-
pied by a patriarch, like Jacob. One of the sub-plots of this volume is
Olds's rewriting of biblical legends to create a place for herself as
acting subject, a place traditionally forbidden to women in these patriarchal tales. It is also intriguing to note that the Apocryphal book
of The Wisdom of Solomon identifies the messenger who struggles

with Jacob as Wisdom, Sophia herself (10:12). In this book, Sophia's power is not shown in physical defeat of the mortal Jacob but in choosing not to exercise such direct power. In this way she enlists him in the greater spiritual enterprise. However, Sophia is acting as an agent of God, who has told her, "Make your dwelling in Jacob, / and in Israel receive your inheritance" (Sirach 24:8). In struggling with her father, Olds may be in essence struggling to release the power of Sophia from patriarchal control. Throughout *The Father*, Olds speaks and acts personally and archetypally at once, on a "transpersonal level" (Woodman 1985).

Olds's progress in this process of surviving and replacing her father is not even. At one point she panics at the thought of receiving the dreaded telephone call before she is ready. But when her father's death is imminent, she knows what to do. She inhales him; she takes him in as an act of inspiration, as if she could receive into herself the soul that escapes his body: "I laid my head on the bed in the path of his breath and breathed it" ("The Last Day," Olds 1992, 32–34). She inhales first his last breaths and then the very smell of his body.

> . . . I had thought the last thing between us
> would be a word, a look, a pressure
> of touch, not that he would be dead
> and I would be bending over him
> smelling him, breathing him in
> as you would breathe the air, deeply, before going into exile.
>
>   ("His Smell," Olds 1992, 38)

This language evokes the story of Eve, who was by some Gnostic accounts Sophia's daughter (Robinson 1977, 172). But in the traditional Genesis story and as expanded in Milton's *Paradise Lost*, Adam receives all benefits of God's inspiration and speech, and Eve receives the word or breath of God only at second hand, from Adam. Here the daughter dares to take her father's breath directly, almost to steal it from his unconscious body, so that she receives the same power and blessing as the son. It is as if the Father has become mortal, has become Adam, and the daughter can now unite with him through his son, rather than suffering the fate of the maligned and subservient Eve:

> . . . I wanted to watch my father die
> because I hated him. Oh, I loved him,

. . . .
his silence had mauled me, I was an Eve
he took and pressed back into clay,

. . . .
and now I watched him be undone and
someone in me gloried in it. . . . (1992, 71)

   After her father's death, Olds is at first offended that the corpse
is treated only as a thing and is not attended constantly, as her father
was before death. The problem seems to be that her father has now
become in physical reality what he always was to her emotionally—an inert body (see "The Dead Body," Olds 1992, 39–40). If
this is true, if the corpse is indeed no more nor less than the presence of her callous father during life, then what, exactly, has she
breathed in? What has she sought to inherit from him? What has she
taken from him, received at his death? The answer seems to lie not
in the peculiar characteristics of this particular father, but in the
symbolic potency, the social power of the Father and in the daughter's feelings of love, awe, hatred, resentment toward that abstract,
symbolic power. She has breathed in the invisible power of his role,
what God first breathed into Adam: his social status as male, as
Father. And since the penis or phallus is usually the symbol of male
dominance in a patriarchy, her breathing in his power ("the cock
in the mouth") is symbolically sexual, incestuous. Two poems from
the second half of the volume, after the father's death, relate that
death to the daughter's sexual intimacy with her husband. In "What
Shocked Me When My Father Died," Olds is stunned to discover
that her mournful sobbing might be misconstrued by others as
moans of sexual pleasure. Yet her earlier poems have prepared for
this sexual union of daughter and father—not a physical but a symbolic union, achieved through the transmission of the father's phallic potency. Even though in the earlier poem "Nullipara" Olds fears
she will never deliver the father she will carry after his death, in reality she bears his inheritance like the fruit Eve plucked from her
Father's tree of knowledge (1992, 42–43).
   Once the father's power has been stolen or inherited, it will not
be lost. As Jung has said of the end of the incest quest, "if the libido
manages to tear itself loose [from the parental imago] and force its
way up again, something like a miracle happens: . . . the libido, apparently dead, wakes to renewed fruitfulness" (Jung 1980, 5:292). In
a poem that seems to gloat over the father's death but actually re-

cords the abrupt relief of a maligned daughter, Olds celebrates the fact that her father can no longer undermine her in his terrible role—that he died when their relations were good, when his last speech was to ask her for a kiss (1992, 52). And on the first anniversary of her father's death, as Olds visits his grave, she discovers that she can now retrieve this power of the Good Father symbolically, almost as some communicants believe they receive the body of Christ in the eucharist: ". . . when I kissed his stone it was not enough, / when I licked it my tongue went dry for a moment, I / ate his dust, I tasted my dirt host" ("One Year," Olds 1992, 54–55). In another parallel to Christian theology, Olds seems to find that the man who gave her life also died for her, and in his death gave her a greater spiritual power on which she can draw internally and repeatedly for sustenance.

The "corpse girl," the clay-embalmed Eve who glories in her father's death—the death of the patriarch and not the victim, the social role and not the person—finds toward the end of this volume that she has now the power to give him speech, to animate the soulless body. Two of the volume's last poems are spoken not by Olds but by her father, first to his cronies in the afterlife and then, in the closing poem of the volume, to his daughter. Both poems affirm not only the father, in giving him speech, but also the daughter as, in a sense, the maker of the father through poetry, the father's pen or potency, so to speak. The daughter is now the writer; she possesses the power of words because of her own ability to work imaginatively within a symbolic system and not because she physically possesses a penis, which has been taken as a symbol for the power of the pen. In "When the Dead Ask My Father About Me" (1992, 73–74), the father at last finds a meaningful vocation in what he has given and still gives to his daughter.

> . . . She could
> speak, you see. As if my own
> jaws, throat, and larynx had come
> alive in her. But all she wanted
> was that dirt from my tongue, umber lump you could
> pass, mouth-to-mouth, she wanted us to
> lie down, in a birth-room, and me
> to labor it out, lever it into her
> mouth I am audible, listen! this is *my* song.

Here is the incestuous scenario again, the daughter desiring a sexual emission from her father. But it is the father who labors and gives birth and the daughter who grows from this birth-gift, and in her growth returns the gift to the giver. Jung supplies some understanding of why Olds craves "that dirt from my tongue" in words reminiscent of Sophia's attempted union with her Father Bythos (the Abyss):

> Wisdom dwells in the depths, the wisdom of the mother [father]; being one with her means being granted a vision of deeper things, of the primordial images and primitive forces which underlie all life and are its nourishing, sustaining, creative matrix. (Jung 1980, 5:413)

The idea of incest must be confronted to be overcome and to achieve a higher end, as Twitchell has said of allusions to incest in pornographic art:

> . . . the idea of the act, the concept of breaching norms and inverting roles, becomes part of a more comprehensive attempt to rend asunder the conventions not just of family life, but of society itself. . . . Incest is the means to the end, not the end in itself. It is the social limit to be sabotaged, the bridge to be burned, so that there can be no turning back to normalcy. (1987, 176, 178)

An advocacy of incest by men, as in pornography, is a regressive move toward social and psychological hoarding that enslaves women to men's desires, especially if it is taken as a literal enactment of the right of males in a patriarchy. The advocacy of symbolic incest by women is an enlightening and advancing move because it breaches the social restrictions on women that determine their subservience in a patriarchy. But Olds also takes care not to harm the individuals involved in this revolutionary process, and she succeeds because she is able to deal with them as symbols rather than as social beings.

Finally, in the volume's last poem, "My Father Speaks to Me from the Dead," (1992, 78–79), Olds hears from her father what she has always needed to hear. She receives his full attention and his direct speech, adult to adult, and what he speaks of is his love for her, with full sensual appreciation of her body and her mind, not shirking the usually tabooed areas.

> . . . I love your our my legs, they are so
> long because they are yours and mine
> both. I love your—what can I call it,
> between your legs, we never named it, the

> glint and purity of its curls.
>
> .   .   .   .
>
> I love your brain, its halves and silvery
> folds, like a woman's labia. . . .

At the same time that he seems to claim her, parentally and even sexually as a lover, at the end of the poem he also releases her from his desire. The desire that he passes on to her is all hers to use for her benefit in her own life, and not a social obligation to him. The incest remains imaginary, verbal, symbolic.

> . . . I am matter,
> your father, I made you, when I say now that I love you
> I mean look down at your hand, move it,
> that action is matter's love, for human
> love go elsewhere.

Because he affirms her as a whole sexual being, this father infuses his daughter with an elemental love that completes her and allows her to live in the world as an equal with all others, not as an empty, partial being dependent on the affirmations of others. As Judith Lewis Herman has put it, "The erotic bond is a precondition for the child's ability to form relationships and a sense of self, and for the development of a basic sense of well-being that will survive the inevitable frustrations and disappointments of life" (Herman and Hirschman 1982, 53). Or, as Woodman puts it, "Psychic incest is the energy source of creativity" (1985, 32). But most notably, this erotically nurturing father is the creation of his daughter, much as Sophia caused the creation of Christ in response to her inability to unite with the Father. And Olds flourishes with the words that come from the father's mouth to affirm her. During and after her father's death, Olds has learned to defeat the Terrible Father and to create and maintain the Good Father, the internal father-muse who reliably and lastingly inspires her with both love and power, so that she might say along with Sophia: "Wisdom praises herself, / and tells of her glory in the midst of her people" (Sirach 24:1).

Conclusion:
Voices Silenced, Voices Raised

For anne sexton and sylvia plath, the allure of incest and their pursuit of union with the father finally resulted in an annihilation of self, as compliance turned to complicity and the father's ultimately inaccessible and more powerful persona demanded capitulation as the only possible form of contact between aspiring daughter and established father. Eventually, the Orphan Annie of this early confessional poetry lost not only her eyes but her sense of self and even her life, her place as a separate being in the world, much as Electra chose to duplicate her father's crime in order to cleave to him. Similarly, Anaïs Nin's abortion, like her affairs with her father and her psychiatrists, is a literal, concrete rendering of the more symbolic experiences presented in the poetry of Sexton and Plath and suggested in the character of Sophocles' Electra. Nin's choice to abort a late-term fetus so that she might continue to serve the men who needed her, and her after-the-fact rationalization of this act, as a reabsorption of the life her body gave rise to, represents an explicit hoarding, a denial of new life by the complicitous daughter in service to the father.

Nin protects herself by using the system to her advantage, but Sexton and Plath remain caught within it. If, as Phyllis Chesler asserts, "Suicide *attempts* are the grand rites of 'femininity'—i.e., women are supposed to 'lose' in order to 'win,'" then the suicide attempts of Plath and Sexton may be seen as perverse efforts to adjust to the system, to reduce themselves to proper size. Successful suicides, however, are a different matter, according to Chesler: "Women who *succeed* at suicide are, tragically, outwitting or rejecting their 'feminine' role, and at the only price possible: their death" (1972, 49). Sexton and Plath were silenced at least in part by their incestuous longings for the distant and powerful father-figure, the demon-lover, and by their inability to develop a paternal muse who would nourish and support their desire to write and grow. In the poems

138

they wrote before their deaths, both Sexton and Plath depict suicide as accomplishing an incestuous union, as an absorption either of self into father (like Electra) or of children into the self (like Nin). But both absorptions involve the death of the individual self. Both Sexton and Plath, after struggling to be accepted and assisted in their own rights as people and as poets, succumbed to the sins of the father—an intolerance of individuality and separation, the choice of incest.

Signs of Sexton's inability to separate from the father-imago occur early in her poetry. In "Where I Live in This Honorable House of the Laurel Tree" (1981, 17–18), a beautiful early poem, Sexton reinterprets the Greek myth of Daphne and her attempted rape by Apollo, father-god of sun and poetry. In the myth, the young nymph Daphne turns into a laurel tree to escape the pursuit of Apollo, father-god. In Sexton's poem, the maiden-tree, millennia later, laments her frustrated desire; her leaves yearn toward the sun (toward Apollo), but no contact results.

> I build the air with the crown of honor; it keys
> my out of time and luckless appetite.
> You gave me honor too soon, Apollo.
> There is no one left who understands
> how I wait
> here in my wooden legs and O
> my green green hands.

The maiden who preserves her virginity, her separateness, who avoids Apollo's right to seduce her, lives through an eternal agony of frustrated desire, unheard loss, and an ironic outward manifestation of honor in the laurel leaves of her canopy—in all, a living death. Sexton's poem suggests not just Daphne's punishment for evading the father's desire but her regrets over her own lost vitality. Father-daughter love is necessary to fuel the emotional growth of the child, as long as the incestuous union remains symbolic and not actual:

> If incest is unrecognized, rejected, repressed, the individual will be left with nothing but the arid, closed field of some abandonment or deadly depression. If incest is overtly practiced and the individual has eyes, ears, and sex only for those closest to him or their surrogates, then he will always be on the verge of fragmentation and breakdown. (Roustang 1984, 101)

But Apollo pressed his love too literally and "too soon," and Daphne resisted a desire that was imposed on her and not developed as her own. The result is a permanent imprisonment, an impotence of desire, an "out of time and luckless appetite," which characterizes the personas of Sexton and Plath.

In another early poem, "The Moss of His Skin" (1981, 26–27), Sexton writes of an old Arabian custom of burying young daughters alive, next to their dead fathers. Again, as in "Where I Live in This Honorable House of the Laurel Tree," this poem is a dramatic monologue, but this time the daughter suffers not from her refusal of the father's right but as the sacrificial indulgence of the father's right—he does not yield his possession of her, even after his death. The poem ends as the girl speaks from within the coffin she shares with her dead father:

> . . . My sisters
> will never know that I fall
> out of myself and pretend
> that Allah will not see
> how I hold my daddy
> like an old stone tree.

This daughter, in a sense, does receive the intimate physical contact with her father that she secretly desires, but only after he has nothing more to give to her life and is just decaying flesh. In neither poem, that of Daphne or that of the buried Arabian girl, does the daughter receive the equal relation, the fair contact with the father that she would desire. These two poems seem to show Sexton's awareness of the irresolvable paradox of the daughter's role: she suffers if she denies or is denied incestuous contact with the father, and she suffers if she actually receives such contact. The daughter is preserved as a living but static object or sacrificed to death; she inherits only a distant light or a decaying body. To the question Yeats asks of Leda after her rape by Zeus—"Did she put on his knowledge with his power . . . ?" (Yeats 1989, 215)—Daphne and the Arabian girl would have to answer No: in each case, the mortal daughter's contact with a dead or distant father brings her loss, estrangement, despair, or death. This seems to be Sexton's ingrained expectation of the results of the daughter's desire for the father. In her poetry, the father is stuck in his Terrible, punitive role, and the daughter is trapped in her role of perpetual victim.

Despite the very negative character of the father-daughter relationship in these early poems, later poems show the ongoing allure
of an incestuous union with a father-figure, even at the expense of
the daughter's individuality. When Sexton turns to God in her later
poems, even this relationship is depicted as incestuous, in the sense
of a monopolizing union much to the father's advantage. "The Rowing Endeth" (1981, 473–74) is the closing poem of *The Awful Rowing
Toward God,* the last volume of poetry published in Sexton's lifetime.
In this poem, Sexton presents herself as arriving at the "island called
God." Conceiving God as a remote island awaiting private discovery,
rather than as the sum of all living things, is a kind of hoarding in
its own right. The image of her arrival is similarly incestuous; she
enters the "flesh of The Island." As in "The Moss of His Skin," the
destitute daughter is finally in contact with her fleshy father. But it
is quite clear that Sexton's persona, for all her rowing, has not completed the incest quest described by Jung—she still seeks the protective physical father and not his spiritual equivalent, even in God
himself. Their encounter takes place in a poker game between Sexton and God, which inevitably God wins.

> Dearest dealer,
> I with my royal straight flush,
> love you so for your wild card,
> that untamable, eternal, gut-driven *ha-ha*
> and lucky love.

Jacques Lacan has characterized the symbolic Father, the absolute
Patriarch who imposes the final necessity of the law against incest,
as "the one who has the master trump and knows it" (1968, 271).
The final poem published in Sexton's lifetime thus echoes the narrator's original assertion to her analyst-father in the first poem of
her first volume: "Of course, I love you" (1981, 3)—I have no
choice! This daughter has made no progress in relation to her
father-imago over the course of the poetic canon. In the first poem
she is infantilized with a smock and moccasins, while in the later
poem she cannot play as well as she might because her awe for her
partner overwhelms her. God's laughter forces itself into her passive
mouth (as opposed to Olds's actively breathing in her father's last
breath), provoking in turn her own laugh: of resignation or despair,
of the absurdity of trying to beat God, the Father, at his own game
and on his own grounds. Sexton preserves an essentially submissive

feminine attitude in her poetic relations to father-figures right to
the end. The only way for Sexton to remove herself from the authority of the father would be to redefine the nature of the father, as
Sharon Olds has done, to humanize and then symbolize him. But
Sexton, with her urgent desire for protection and affirmation from
a Daddy, could not do this.

   One other poem by Sexton illustrates almost painfully the daughter's compulsion toward incest. It is clear from the first lines of "Divorce, Thy Name Is Woman" (1981, 545–46) that the Daddy of the
poem is not the actual father.

> I am divorcing daddy—Dybbuk! Dybbuk!
> I have been doing it daily all my life
> since his sperm left him
> drilling upwards and stuck to an egg.

It is quite interesting to note here the difference between Sharon
Olds conceiving of her own sperm as active and orgasmic and part
of her own vitality, and Sexton here speaking of "his sperm," which
has "left him." Sexton does not seize and possess her own origins as
Olds does, and since her father continues to live inside her as her
progenitor, Sexton cannot separate from him emotionally either.
Thus when she refers to her own conception, Sexton characterizes
this Daddy as a dybbuk—the spirit of a dead person that invades and
possesses another living body. The Daddy is not an actual, living person, but the father-imago carried in the daughter's head, the pervasive father-figure that will not die and let the daughter live her own
life—the Terrible Father, the demon-lover, what Esther Harding
calls the "ghostly lover":

> In [the Jewish] legend [of the dybbuk] the lover who lures his beloved
> away from reality into union with himself is shown quite objectively as
> the ghost of a dead youth with whom the heroine was in love. . . . [S]he
> is entirely absorbed in him and by him. She is lost to the real world about
> her, for she is living only in her own subjective world with her ghostly
> lover. (1970, 37)

Since Sexton's father-imago has not fulfilled the daughter's needs
and wants, but takes credit for her very existence, he remains em-
bedded within her psyche as a denying and demeaning force.

   However, the speaker still projects her psychic struggles to gain
some nurture and assistance from this dybbuk as if they were real

external events—perhaps because the consequences of such struggles in her life are quite real.

> Daddy and his whiskey breath
> made a long midnight visit
> in a dream that is not a dream
> and then called his lawyer quickly.
> Daddy divorcing me.

The invasion of the dybbuk is presented as an incestuous act, but the result is a social separation of father from daughter that also ensures the daughter's inability ever to separate emotionally from the father, much as Sexton's Daphne cannot quit her longings for the father-god she lost in fleeing his invasive desire. This is the stuff of dreams, of the psyche, but also of life, of reality—"dream that is not a dream"—for the daughter's impotence to divorce her father-imago, as the real father has "divorced" or rejected her, leads to her submissive relations with all paternal figures in society. She remains haunted by the patriarchal figure in her head who has used her to gratify himself and then rejected her without meeting her needs, leaving her with neither power nor knowledge, much less love. Sexton's speaker is finally powerless to evict the internal father, because her own need and learned subjection overpower any dignifying anger. She can only seek another consummation with him, even though that necessarily entails, dybbuk that he is, her own dissolution.

> . . . I am pacing the bedroom.
> . . . .
> waiting, waiting for Daddy to come home
> and stuff me so full of our infected child
> that I turn invisible, but married,
> at last.

Like Anne Sexton, Sylvia Plath shows at the end of her poetic career a failure to separate from the father and thrive on her own as an independent being. Also like Sexton, part of the allure of this incestuous union for Plath is the freedom from responsibility it seems to grant. The daughter in a bonded relationship with the father can rely on him to direct her life; she is therefore unformed and unaccountable. Plath says as much in "Little Fugue" (1981, 187–88), which is narrated from the viewpoint of a young child. The father is presented as all-powerful and also guilty, and this extreme portrayal leaves the child in a state of moral nonbeing.

> . . . Such a dark funnel, my father!
> I see your voice
>
> .   .   .   .
> A yew hedge of orders,
> Gothic and barbarous, pure German.
> Dead men cry from it.
> I am guilty of nothing.
>
> .   .   .   .
> I was seven, I knew nothing.
> The world occurred.
>
> .   .   .   .
> I survive the while. . . .

One advantage of the demon-lover, the all-powerful Daddy who absorbs and controls the thoughts and acts of the daughter, is that this absolute being excuses the daughter from social responsibilities. It is interesting to note that "fugue" is not only a musical piece but also a psychological term denoting a lapse of memory or consciousness, a confused awareness of present realities, a failure to be presently accountable.

Feminists since Plath have identified this extreme image of the father as a great danger to the viability of the daughter, and have recently worked to reduce the paternal imago to more manageable and human proportions. Rich has commented on this problem in the poetry of Plath and has also pointed out a way beyond:

> It strikes me that in the work . . . Man appears as, if not a dream, a fascination and a terror; and that the source of the fascination and the terror is, simply, Man's power—to dominate, tyrannize, choose, or reject the woman. The charisma of Man seems to come purely from his power over her and his control of the world by force, not from anything fertile or life-giving in him. And . . . it is finally the woman's sense of *herself*—embattled, possessed—that gives the poetry its dynamic charge, its rhythms of struggle, need, will, and female energy. (1979, 36)

The danger of the Terrible Father is in the absolute evil and opposition of his image. The potential for a woman's salvation lies in her ability to focus on her own image and take what she needs from him to sustain her own life, rather than envying his power and lamenting her inevitable subservience (and thereby preserving the relationship). As Jung says of the individual on the incest quest, and as we have seen in the Gnostic story of Sophia, the daughter must turn from the power of the Terrible Father in order to preserve herself and create an image of the Good Father, which will nurture and encourage her in her growth and desires.

If, on the other hand, the father-imago is not used to excuse the desires and responsibilities of the daughter, he may be used to enforce the daughter's victimization. The Terrible Father's one-sided evil nature demands an unrealistically good, innocent victim for its own self-definition and consumption. "Daddy" (Plath 1981, 222–24) is built, undeniably, on many personal details, both from Plath's relationship with her father and from her marriage. Elizabeth Butler Cullingford (1989) has also written a compelling analysis of "Daddy" and other Plath poems as a poetic daughter's response to the patriarchal expectations of a poetic father, W. B. Yeats, in whose former home Plath died. Plath herself once introduced "Daddy" as "spoken by a girl with an Electra complex. Her father died while she thought he was God" (1981, 293 n. 183). But the real interest of the poem is in how Plath converts these autobiographical details into an archetypal experience of evil and good, perpetrator and victim, Nazi and Jew. Also of interest is the torturous tension between hatred for this evil father-figure and the fascination of joining his game. The poem begins defiantly, with the speaker seeming to reject the father:

> . . . Daddy, I have had to kill you.
> You died before I had time—
> Marble-heavy, a bag full of God.
>
> . . . .
> I never could talk to you.
> The tongue stuck in my jaw.
>
> It stuck in a barb wire snare.
> Ich, ich, ich, ich,
> I could hardly speak.
> I thought every German was you.
> And the language obscene
>
> An engine, an engine
> Chuffing me off like a Jew.

Jacqueline Rose (226) reveals that earlier typescripts of "Daddy" use the word "incestuous" where "obscene" appears above, and in-

deed, the poem soon moves away from rejection of the despised oppressor and toward a fascination and complicity with him.

> Every woman adores a Fascist,
> The boot in the face, the brute
> Brute heart of a brute like you.
>
> . . . .
>
> I made a model of you,
> A man in black with a Meinkampf look
>
> And a love of the rack and the screw.
> And I said I do, I do.
> So daddy, I'm finally through. . . .

The ending of the poem embodies the torment of the speaker's
split between her identification with the father and her desire for
independence from him. The final "Daddy, daddy, you bastard, I'm
through" can be read both as the disgusted dismissal of the evil
father-figure and as the loss of self that, for the compliant daughter,
ensues from loss of the father. The speaker is tied too closely to her
internal father, her demon-lover, to separate from him, dismiss him,
and establish her own independent existence. She clings to him precisely because he has deprived her of what she needs, and she has in
turn assumed parts of him within herself. To escape this Terrible
Father, Plath's poetic persona tries on the innocence of the Jew in
relation to the Nazi, thus characterizing the political oppression of
females by males, but this dichotomy leads inevitably to the destruction of both. Notably, it is not Plath's speaker who apparently kills
the vampire-father, but the "villagers." She seeks the support and
approval of the community for her innocence and desire to be free
of the oppressor, much like Electra. But his death leads to her end
all the same, because the father killed is the internal Daddy, a father-
imago within her own psyche, and not the real-world father. Cullingford identifies this internal Daddy as "Death-the-Father himself"
and as the "father-Muse" (1989, 251). Surely the father-muse is what
many female poets seek, but not in the form of the consuming Terrible Father. The result of this negative artist-muse relationship is denial of the self, the daughter's patriarchal role in serving the father's
will.

> If the Dracula figure has drunk her blood for seven years, then she, too,
> is doomed to become a vampire. . . . Thus the cycle of oppression and

revenge is self-perpetuating, never ending. The persona begins as a willing victim and ends as a malevolent torturer. . . . Plath's poem shows that to engage male structures of dominance on their own terms is inevitably to be reabsorbed into the destructive patriarchal system. (Cullingford 1989, 254–55)

In her discussion of "Little Fugue" and "Daddy," Rose points out another dimension to the speaker's relation to her father in these poems—the silence of the father toward the daughter, which threatens to silence the daughter as well, by depriving her of access to the personal and social history that should be transmitted through him (1991, 220–21). The language is "obscene" or "incestuous" because it is the language of identification with a Terrible Father, the father who absorbs the child into his own needs and fails to meet hers. To Rose, this is part of the paradox of the Oedipal situation, in that the father commands the child to yield what she cannot yield without losing her identity (228). The Oedipal situation cannot be resolved by the daughter, who, unlike the son, cannot be like the father and have the mother in the symbolic form of his wife. What identity, what genuine speech, is left to the daughter when she is asked to give up an intimate love for her mother and transfer her desires to her father, taking on his own desires as her own? She gropes even to say "I" in a native language.

Plath's final poem is "Edge" (1981, 272–73), which she wrote a week before killing herself (Stevenson 1989, 298). As the title suggests, the poem depicts a mental state on the edge of annihilation, and that state includes an incestuous experience once again—this time with the speaker's children. In lines quite reminiscent of Anaïs Nin's rationalization of her abortion as a reabsorption of her own daughter back into her body, Plath describes the way a dying woman repossesses her children.

> . . . Each dead child coiled, a white serpent,
> One at each little
>
> Pitcher of milk, now empty.
> She has folded
>
> Them back into her body as petals
> Of a rose close when the garden
>
> Stiffens and colors bleed
> From the sweet, deep throats of the night flower.

In this final poetic act, Plath's persona, the dead woman (unlike the historical Plath), reabsorbs her children before extinguishing her own life. This is an act of incest, a refusal to allow her children to live independently of her, and a refusal to extend herself into the future and away from her own paternal origins. The demon-father is not mentioned in this poem, but he is there, for the actions of this woman mirror the greedy, hoarding behavior of the demon-father in poems like "Daddy." "The woman is perfected" in mirroring the behavior of the perfectionistic demon-father. She has become statue-like—"Her dead // Body wears the smile of accomplishment, / The illusion of a Greek necessity // Flows in the scrolls of her toga," reminiscent of the earlier father-colossus. Like Electra, she repeats the father's crime and succumbs to his power, rather than merging his social power with her individual desire to achieve a truly creative result. This may even be an image of Plath becoming her own Terrible Mother, companion to the Terrible Father from whom she cannot separate.

☞

The saving alternative to the fates of Sexton and Plath would be what Jung calls the "sacrifice . . . the very reverse of regression" (Jung 1980, 5:263). Jung refers to a sacrifice of personal possession, a surrender of the primacy of protective emotional relations with one's parents in particular—a chosen emotional reduction from the status of favorite to the acceptance of being one of many, akin to Lacan's goal of enlightened castration. The countervailing temptation is the encompassing reassurance of an ultimate Power, of God, even if one also fights against it, like a young child battling the parent she knows she depends on. In Lacan's philosophy, "the need, the desire, the wish for the Phallus is great. No matter how oppressive its reign, it is much more comforting than no one in command" (Gallop 1982, 130–31). The negative impulse toward incest arises from the desire to secure the protection from challenge and frustration such a relationship affords. But if the literal hoarding of emotional relationships, real or desired, can be overcome, a wealth of symbolic relations are possible. The relationship with the father is Terrible or demonic when the possessive child evokes the image of the possessive, consuming parent; the symbolic relationship is Good or spiritual when the child's nonpossessive love evokes a freeing love in return, as we have seen in Sharon Olds's relations with her symbolic father. What Olds achieves is an ability to allow the physical father to die—not only to die physically but to die away from her as well. She lets go of his potentially comforting but also limiting presence internally, and for that reason she can proceed with his symbolic representation. Thus Olds creates an affirmative but fragmentary father—not a whole, demonic being who exercises his own will, but a collection of images that supply the daughter with what she needs.

To move beyond the psychic stage of childhood requires the psychic death of the parents, as Jung has explained:

> For when such a vitally important figure as the ideal is about to change, it is as though that figure had to die. . . . [A]ny growing beyond oneself means death. . . . It is a decision in favour of life, at whose end death stands. Love and death have not a little to do with one another. (Jung 1980, 5:285)

Indeed, the death of the literal incest impulse, in the sense of cleaving to the father, liberates for the grown daughter the father's symbolic power. To put it another way, when the daughter no longer clings to the comfort and protection she imagines she might receive from the father and risks her own immersion in the chancy flux of life, she assumes for herself all the power the father in actuality (free of social illusions) ever had—that of standing on her own and caring for herself. The transition from tyrannical, possessing father to enabling father parallels the transition of the daughter from a painfully restricted submission to personal empowerment. In an absolute sense, the daughter doesn't possess the phallus any more than her father did, but then neither does she assume her dispossession either. The right mental balance is a simultaneous symbolic possession and literal dispossession: "knowingly, lucidly to exercise and *and* [*sic*] criticize power is to dephallicize, to assume the phallus and unveil that assumption as presumption, as fraud. A constantly double discourse is necessary, one that asserts and then questions" (Gallop 1982, 122). The problem that Rich has raised is how both men and women will actively and voluntarily engage in this "double discourse" in a patriarchal society that rewards males for taking their phallic power literally.

Caitlin Matthews suggests that the repressed and resurrected goddess Sophia, in all her positive and negative manifestations, symbolizes woman's potential to evolve against the odds.

For women, Sophia is a powerful archetype for identification on many levels. She is every woman ever raped, denied her creativity, kept isolated, abandoned or exiled. She is also potentially within all women who wish to discover their creativity, maintain their integrity, and support justice in the world and in themselves. She is the strong woman who survives in the face of adversity and rescues her treasures, to display them at a more suitable time. As Sophia emerges further into consciousness, so will the image of the empowered woman become apparent in the world. (1992, 331)

This gradual coming to consciousness of an enabling and healing archetype is what Jung has identified as the goal of the incest quest—a new sense of self larger than the ego, a sense of self that is both individual and spiritual, both one alone and one of many. Neumann has called this archetype the "guiding Sophia-Self" (Neumann 1971, 128). Juliet Mitchell has envisioned a similar task for women who desire freedom from patriarchal limitations: the creative transformation of the contents of the psyche into positive, empowering images of woman and her role in society (1974, 415), images that can counter and revise the punitive male, phallic images. Mary Daly has anticipated the coming of an Antichrist in the form of the female power that has been excluded from the masculine, Christian God:

The Antichrist dreaded by the patriarchs may be the surge of consciousness, the spiritual awakening, that can bring us beyond Christolatry into a fuller stage of conscious participation in the *living* God.

Seen from this perspective the Antichrist and the *Second Coming of women* are synonymous. The Second Coming is not a return of Christ but a new arrival of female presence, once strong and powerful, but enchained since the dawn of patriarchy. . . . Far from being a "return" to the past, it implies a qualitative leap toward psychic androgyny. The new arrival of female presence is the necessary catalyst for this leap. (1973, 96–97)

Such a lifting of the dread of punishment for women and men daring to be whole is akin to the liberation of being that for women comes with daring to imagine incest. The poetry of Olds and other women writing now suggests that the images arising from the unconscious minds of women in response to patriarchy are already becoming androgynous. We have seen how Olds feminizes her father-imago and assumes many traditionally masculine powers and prerogatives. Likewise, several contemporary women poets have imagined such androgynous unity as a phallic womb. In Lucille Clifton's poem "Mary," Jesus's mother, in a sexual rapture, has a garden sprout from her mouth and a tree appear between her legs (Clifton 1987, 99). Clifton's poem empowers Mary in seeing her not as the passive, virginal vessel of God's power but the sexually conscious partner of the Father; Mary's awareness of the incestuous act allows her to visualize herself as giving birth to nature. In many ways this poem presents the daughter's dilemma in a patriarchal society: to be used as the vessel of the father's unconscious desires, or to be conscious of those desires and of her own, and to use them to create more of the world she lives in. The principle of strength and power in the male, symbolized by the phallus, when held within the creative wholeness of the woman, is a symbol of consummation for women. The woman then is not the delivering vessel of man's patriarchal power; rather, the man is the internal empowerment of the creative function of the woman. The male is muse to the female creator, ink in the female pen. This fusion of traditionally masculine and feminine images becomes possible when these human qualities are no longer restricted to their supposedly appropriate sexes and when women and men realize that they must embody a wholeness of being—they must, in effect, possess a phallic womb (Woodman 1993, 2). In the Gnostic story of Sophia, Christ gives form to Sophia's passion, Achamoth, but he does so to enable that passion or intuition, rather than to enslave it. Christ brings Achamoth into full being, in opposition to the more traditional situation of the male poet inspired by his female muse.

Gilbert and Gubar have discussed the traditional literary relation of male and female in terms of the literary theory of Harold Bloom.

Bloom's model of literary history is intensely (even exclusively) male, and necessarily patriarchal. For this reason it has seemed, and no doubt will continue to seem, offensively sexist to some feminist critics. Not only, after all, does Bloom describe literary history as the crucial warfare of fathers and sons, he sees Milton's fiercely masculine fallen Satan as *the* type of the poet in our culture. And he metaphorically defines the poetic process as a sexual encounter between a male poet and his female muse. Where, then, does the female poet fit in? Does she want to annihilate a "forefather" or a "foremother"? What if she can find no models, no precursors? Does she have a muse, and what is its sex? (Gilbert and Gubar 1979, 47)

Ironically, Milton's Satan himself initiates a woman into his society, and Eve acts with this power, perhaps becoming "*the* type of the [female] poet in our culture." For Eve steals the fruit of the Father, the power of the Father, the seed on his phallic tree. With this new knowledge she suffers, certainly, and has to acknowledge her own castration, as Lacan would have it. But again, as with Sophia, the greater good is achieved only by a daughter's transgression, which is perceived at first as treacherous but which opens up the closed patriarchal system. One might also say that Eve's muse was Satan, who led her to the power he had and she did not, who was willing to share that power with a woman. Satan is a precursor of the father-muse.

As Lynda Boose has written, Eve's confrontation with God is the crux of the incest quest.

> Eve's seizure of the Father's seed is mythically analogous to an act of incest. . . . Read through its family structures, the text describes the father's (unacknowledged) seduction of his daughter and the daughter's punished reach for love and union with the all-powerful and distant parent. (Boose 1989, 55–56)

Boose believes that the outcome of the story is pessimistic, that Eve's punishment indicates her subordination in the patriarchal system. She receives the fruit only to pass it on to Adam, thus becoming "the (empty) medium through which male authority is passed from father to son, her aggressive right to possess it converted into the passive right to transmit it" (Boose 1989, 55). But Eve in her action of defiance plucks the treasure from the realm of the Terrible Father (as Jung describes the positive goal of the incest quest). She not only creates her own identity as an individual but opens up the closed system of Eden, initiates the creation of humanity, and determines the coming of Christ, very much in line with the effects of Sophia's transgression against Bythos.

What Sophia does, Achamoth repeats. What Achamoth does, Eve repeats. What Eve does, many women poets and more and more women in traditional life pursuits are now doing, by plucking images of self-possession from the unconscious realm and using them to create new myths that clarify and expand the woman's self. Page Du-Bois (1991) has shown that ancient female images of power and self-sufficiency, like that of the earth as a spontaneously fertile female being, were once revised by Plato and others to reduce them to male control. In male minds, the earth became a barren field whose fertility depended on plowing and seeding by men. This human action of taming the natural fertility of the female clearly parallels the story of Adam and Eve's expulsion from an all-giving paradise, at the direction of God. But the biblical Apocrypha presents an image of Wisdom or Sophia, the female element of the godhead, which directly and stunningly contradicts the actions of the punitive God in Genesis. Wisdom says:

> Come to me, you who desire me,
>   and eat your fill of my fruits.
> . . . .
> those who eat of me will hunger for more,
>   and those who drink of me will thirst for more. (Sirach 24:19, 21)

The plenitude of the female is still available to compensate for the hoarding and denial of the male God. If such a change in literary and psychic imagery from female abundance and generosity to male power and control has occurred, a return to female images of strength and abundance is also possible. Sappho can speak again.

The poetry of Anne Sexton, Sylvia Plath, Adrienne Rich, and Sharon Olds suggests that women in the last few decades have been on a quest to identify their own sources of strength and fertility and to retrieve them from male appropriation, to wrest the woman's self free of the limiting Terrible Father by means of imagining and redefining incest. It is not that Freud and psychoanalysis are dead or dying, as *Time* has suggested, but that some of the techniques that Freud advocated and psychoanalysis has made available to the public are being used by women to free themselves from social strictures that Freud took for granted as part of female nature. Sexton and Plath exposed to conscious view the great pain and anguish accompanying the images of self that women carry unconsciously within a patriarchy; Rich strongly rejected those images as not acceptable for women, and Olds and others have begun the process of revising those images and conceiving newly positive images of strength and wholeness. It may well be that the current "plague" of recovered memories of incest in adult women is not some dire disease in those women (though it may be for patriarchal institutions), but that such memories represent another stage in the quest towards repossessing the strong self in women, much as we have seen in the works of these four poets. Perhaps the quest, which was available previously only to poets able to plumb the unconscious mind, is now strong enough to assert itself in more conscious forms, such as in recovered memories of incest. If so, these poets should provide some guidance to those who have joined them on the incest quest.

Bibliography

Acocella, Joan. 1998. *Creating Hysteria*. New York: Jossey-Bass.

Ayres, B. Drummond, Jr. 1994. "Jury Awards Father Who Challenged 'Memory' Therapy." *New York Times*, 22 May, late ed., A1 +.

Bachofen, J. J. 1973. *Myth, Religion, and Mother Right*. Translated by Ralph Manheim. Bollingen Series, no. 84. Princeton: Princeton University Press.

Boose, Lynda E. 1989. "The Father's House and the Daughter in It: The Structures of Western Culture's Daughter-Father Relationship." In Boose and Flowers, 19–74.

Boose, Lynda E., and Betty S. Flowers, eds. 1989. *Daughters and Fathers*. Baltimore: Johns Hopkins University Press.

Cady, Susan, Marian Ronan, and Hal Taussig. 1986. *Sophia: The Future of Feminist Spirituality*. New York: Harper & Row.

Campbell, Joseph. 1973. *Myths to Live By*. New York: Bantam.

Caruth, Cathy. 1996. *Unclaimed Experience: Trauma, Narrative, and History*. Baltimore: Johns Hopkins University Press.

Champagne, Rosaria. 1996. *The Politics of Survivorship: Incest, Women's Literature, and Feminist Theory*. New York: New York University Press.

Chesler, Phyllis. 1972. *Women and Madness*. New York: Doubleday.

Christ, Carol, and Judith Plaskow. 1979. Introduction to *Womanspirit Rising: A Feminist Reader in Religion,* ed. Carol Christ and Judith Plaskow, 1–17. New York: Harper & Row.

Clegg, Christine. 1999. "Feminist Recoveries in *My Father's House*." *Feminist Review* 61 (spring): 67–82.

Clifton, Lucille. 1987. *Good Woman*. Brockport, N.Y.: BOA Editions.

Crews, Frederick, et al. 1997. *The Memory Wars: Freud's Legacy in Dispute*. New York: New York Review.

Cullingford, Elizabeth Butler. 1989. "A Father's Prayer, a Daughter's Anger: W. B. Yeats and Sylvia Plath." In Boose and Flowers, 233–55.

Cutting, Linda Katherine. 1993. "Give and Take." *New York Times Magazine*, 31 October, 52 +.

Daly, Mary. 1973. *Beyond God the Father*. Boston: Beacon.

DeJean, Joan. 1989. *Fictions of Sappho, 1546–1937*. Chicago: University of Chicago Press.

DuBois, Page. 1991. Introduction to *Love Songs* by Sappho, translated by Paul Roche. New York: Signet.

155

Durkheim, Emile. 1963. *Incest: The Nature and Origin of the Taboo.* Translated by Edward Sagarin. New York: Lyle Stuart.

Elmer-DeWitt, Philip. 1993. "Too Violent for Kids?" *Time,* 27 September, 70–71.

Engelsman, Joan Chamberlain. 1979. *The Feminine Dimension of the Divine.* Philadelphia: Westminster.

Freud, Sigmund. 1957. *The Standard Edition of the Complete Psychological Works.* Translated by James Strachey. 23 vols. London: Hogarth.

Froula, Christine. 1989. "The Daughter's Seduction: Sexual Violence and Literary History." In Boose and Flowers, 111–135.

Gallop, Jane. 1982. *The Daughter's Seduction: Feminism and Psychoanalysis.* Ithaca: Cornell University Press.

Gilbert, Sandra M., and Susan Gubar. 1979. *The Madwoman in the Attic: The Woman Writer and the Nineteenth-Century Literary Imagination.* New Haven: Yale University Press.

Gray, Paul. 1993. "The Assault on Freud." *Time,* 29 November, 47–51.

Harding, M. Esther. 1970. *The Way of All Women: A Psychological Interpretation.* New York: Putnam.

Heilbrun, Carolyn G. 1982. *Toward a Recognition of Androgyny.* New York: Norton.

Herman, Judith Lewis. 1992. *Trauma and Recovery.* New York: Basic.

Herman, Judith Lewis, with Lisa Hirschman. 1982. *Father-Daughter Incest.* Cambridge: Harvard University Press.

Irenaeus. 1953. "Against Heresies." In *The Ante-Nicene Fathers: Translations of the Writings of the Fathers Down to A.D. 325,* ed. Alexander Roberts and James Donaldson, 1:315–567. Grand Rapids, Mich.: Eerdmans.

Jaroff, Leon. 1993. "Lies of the Mind." *Time,* 29 November, 52–59.

Jung, C. G. 1965. *Memories, Dreams, Reflections.* Edited by Aniela Jaffe. Rev. ed. Translated by Richard and Clara Winston. New York: Vintage.

———. 1980. *Collected Works.* Translated by R. F. C. Hull. 20 vols. Bollingen Series, no. 20. Princeton: Princeton University Press.

Kavaler-Adler, Susan. 1993. *The Compulsion to Create: A Psychoanalytic Study of Women Artists.* New York: Routledge.

Kowaleski-Wallace, Beth. 1989. "Reading the Father Metaphorically." In Yaeger and Kowaleski-Wallace, 296–311.

Kumin, Maxine. 1981. "How It Was." In *Complete Poems,* by Anne Sexton, xix–xxxiv.

Lacan, Jacques. 1968. *Speech and Language in Psychoanalysis.* Translated by Anthony Wilden. Baltimore: Johns Hopkins University Press.

Lévi-Strauss, Claude. 1956. "The Family." In *Man, Culture, and Society,* ed. Harry L. Shapiro, 261–85. New York: Oxford University Press.

———. 1969. *The Elementary Structures of Kinship.* Rev. ed. Translated by J. H. Bell et al. Boston: Beacon.

Malcolm, Janet. 1984. *In the Freud Archives.* New York: Knopf.

———. 1994. *The Silent Woman: Sylvia Plath and Ted Hughes.* New York: Knopf.

Masson, Jeffrey Moussaieff. 1984. *The Assault on Truth: Freud's Suppression of the Seduction Theory.* New York: Farrar, Straus & Giroux.

Matthews, Caitlin. 1992. *Sophia, Goddess of Wisdom: The Divine Feminine from Black Goddess to World Soul.* London: Aquarian.

McLennan, Karen Jacobsen, ed. 1996. *Nature's Ban: Women's Incest Literature.* Boston: Northeastern University Press.

Metzger, Bruce M., and Roland E. Murphy, eds. 1991. *New Oxford Annotated Bible, with the Apocryphal/Deuterocanonical Books.* New York: Oxford University Press.

Middlebrook, Diane Wood. 1991. *Anne Sexton: A Biography.* Boston: Houghton Mifflin.

Mitchell, Juliet. 1974. *Psychoanalysis and Feminism.* New York: Random House.

Nabokov, Vladimir. *Lolita.* 1989. New York: Vintage.

Neumann, Erich. 1963. *The Great Mother: An Analysis of the Archetype.* 2d ed. Translated by Ralph Manheim. Bollingen Series, no. 47. Princeton: Princeton University Press.

—. 1971. *Amor and Psyche: The Psychic Development of the Feminine, A Commentary on the Tale by Apuleius.* Translated by Ralph Manheim. Bollingen Series, no. 54. Princeton: Princeton University Press.

Nin, Anaïs. 1992. *Incest: From "A Journal of Love," The Unexpurgated Diary of Anaïs Nin, 1932–1934.* New York: Harcourt Brace Jovanovich.

Olds, Sharon. 1980. *Satan Says.* Pittsburgh: University of Pittsburgh Press.

—. 1984. *The Dead and the Living.* New York: Knopf.

—. 1987. *The Gold Cell.* New York: Knopf.

—. 1992. *The Father.* New York: Knopf.

—. 1995. *The Wellspring.* New York: Knopf.

—. 1999. *Blood, Tin, Straw.* New York: Knopf.

Pagels, Elaine. 1989. *The Gnostic Gospels.* New York: Vintage.

Perkins, John. 1992. *The Forbidden Self: Symbolic Incest and the Journey Within.* Boston: Shambala.

Plath, Sylvia. 1966. Interview by Peter Orr. In *The Poet Speaks: Interviews with Contemporary Poets.* Ed. Peter Orr, 167–72. London: Routledge and Kegan Paul.

—. 1979. *Johnny Panic and the Bible of Dreams: Short Stories, Prose, and Diary Extracts.* New York: Harper & Row.

—. 1981. *The Collected Poems.* Edited by Ted Hughes. New York: Harper & Row.

—. 1982. *The Journals.* Edited by Ted Hughes and Frances McCullough. New York: Dial.

Rank, Otto. 1992. *The Incest Theme in Literature and Legend: Fundamentals of a Psychology of Literary Creation.* Translated by Gregory C. Richter. Baltimore: Johns Hopkins University Press.

Reich, Walter. 1994. "The Monster in the Mists." *New York Times Book Review,* 15 May, 1+.

Rich, Adrienne. 1973. *Diving into the Wreck.* New York: Norton.

—. 1976. *Of Woman Born: Motherhood as Experience and Institution.* New York: Norton.

—. 1978. *The Dream of a Common Language.* New York: Norton.

————. 1979. *On Lies, Secrets, and Silence: Selected Prose, 1966–1978.* New York: Norton.

————. 1981. *A Wild Patience Has Taken Me This Far.* New York: Norton.

————. 1986a. *Blood, Bread, and Poetry: Selected Prose, 1979–1985.* New York: Norton.

————. 1986b. *Your Native Land, Your Life.* New York: Norton.

————. 1989. *Time's Power.* New York, Norton.

————. 1991. *An Atlas of the Difficult World.* New York: Norton.

————. 1993a. *Collected Early Poems, 1950–1970.* New York: Norton.

————. 1993b. *Poetry and Prose.* 2d ed. Edited by Barbara Charlesworth Gelpi and Albert Gelpi. New York: Norton.

————. 1993c. *What Is Found There: Notebooks on Poetry and Politics.* New York: Norton.

————. 1995. *Dark Fields of the Republic.* New York: Norton.

————. 1999. *Midnight Salvage.* New York: Norton.

Robinson, James M., ed. 1977. *Nag Hammadi Library in English.* Translated by members of the Coptic Gnostic Library Project of the Institute for Antiquity and Christianity. New York: Harper & Row.

Rose, Jacqueline. 1991. *The Haunting of Sylvia Plath.* Cambridge: Harvard University Press.

Roustang, François. 1984. "Uncertainty." Translated by Richard Miller. *October* 28 (spring): 91–103.

Rubin, Gayle. 1975. "The Traffic in Women: Notes on the 'Political Economy' of Sex." In *Toward an Anthropology of Women,* ed. Rayna Reiter, 157–210. New York: Monthly Review.

Russell, Diana E. H. 1986. *The Secret Trauma: Incest in the Lives of Girls and Women.* New York: Basic.

Sappho. 1991. *Love Songs.* Translated by Paul Roche. New York: Signet.

Sexton, Anne. 1981. *Complete Poems.* Boston: Houghton Mifflin.

————. 1985. *No Evil Star: Selected Essays, Interviews, and Prose.* Edited by Steven E. Colburn. Ann Arbor: University of Michigan Press.

Sexton, Linda Gray. 1994. *Searching for Mercy Street: My Journey Back to My Mother, Anne Sexton.* Boston: Little, Brown.

Shengold, Leonard. 1989. *Soul Murder: The Effects of Childhood Abuse and Deprivation.* New Haven: Yale University Press.

Showalter, Elaine. 1997. *Hystories: Hysterical Epidemics and Modern Culture.* New York: Columbia University Press.

Skorczewski, Dawn. 1996. "What Prison Is This?: Literary Critics Cover Incest in Anne Sexton's 'Briar Rose.'" *Signs* 21 (winter): 309–42.

Sophocles. 1994. *Electra.* In *Ajax, Electra, Oedipus Tyrannus,* ed. and trans. Hugh Lloyd-Jones. Cambridge: Harvard University Press.

Spillers, Hortense J. 1989. "'The Permanent Obliquity of an In[pha]llibly Straight': In the Time of the Daughters and Fathers." In Boose and Flowers, 157–76.

Stanley, Alessandra. 1991. "Poet Told All; Therapist Provides the Record." *New York Times,* 15 July, 1 + .

Stevenson, Anne. 1989. *Bitter Fame: A Life of Sylvia Plath.* Boston: Houghton Mifflin.

Tavris, Carol. 1993. "Beware the Incest-Survivor Machine." *New York Times Book Review*, 3 January, 1+.

Twitchell, James B. 1987. *Forbidden Partners: The Incest Taboo in Modern Culture.* New York: Columbia University Press.

Wilson, Elizabeth A. 1999. "Not in This House: Incest, Denial, and Doubt in the White Middle-Class Family." In *Confessional Politics: Women's Sexual Self-Representations in Life Writing and Popular Media,* ed. Irene Gammel, 81–98. Carbondale: Southern Illinois University Press.

Wolff, Charlotte. 1971. *Love Between Women.* New York: St. Martin's.

Woodman, Marion. 1985. *The Pregnant Virgin: A Process of Psychological Transformation.* Toronto: Inner City.

———. 1993. *Leaving My Father's House: A Journey to Conscious Femininity.* Boston: Shambala.

Wright, Lawrence. 1994. *Remembering Satan.* New York: Knopf.

Yaeger, Patricia. 1989. "The Father's Breasts." In Yaeger and Kowaleski-Wallace, 3–21.

Yaeger, Patricia, and Beth Kowalski-Wallace, eds. 1989. *Refiguring the Father: New Feminist Readings of Patriarchy.* Carbondale: Southern Illinois University Press, 1989.

Yeats, W. B. 1989. *The Poems.* Vol. 1 of *The Collected Works.* Rev. ed. Edited by Richard S. Finneran. New York: Macmillan.

Index